MAD DOG SKi

Tignes

A Mad Dog Ski resort guide

Second edition 2008
Published by Mad Dog Ski
maddogski.com

Mad Dog Ski
Tignes
Second edition 2008

Published by Mad Dog Ski
Maps © Mad Dog Ski

Edited by: Gaby de Pace
Design: David Marshall
Artwork: Paddi Graphics
Printed by: Etrinsic

ISBN 978-0-955121524

A catalogue record of this book is available at the British Library.

Mad Dog Ski, PO Box 6321, Bournemouth, BH1 9ED, UK
info@maddogski.com
maddogski.com
+44 (0) 845 054 2906

Contents

About Mad Dog Ski

About Tignes

Planning your trip

On the piste

Food and drink

Other things to do

Children

The list

Maps

About Mad Dog resort guides and how they'll make a real difference to your holiday.

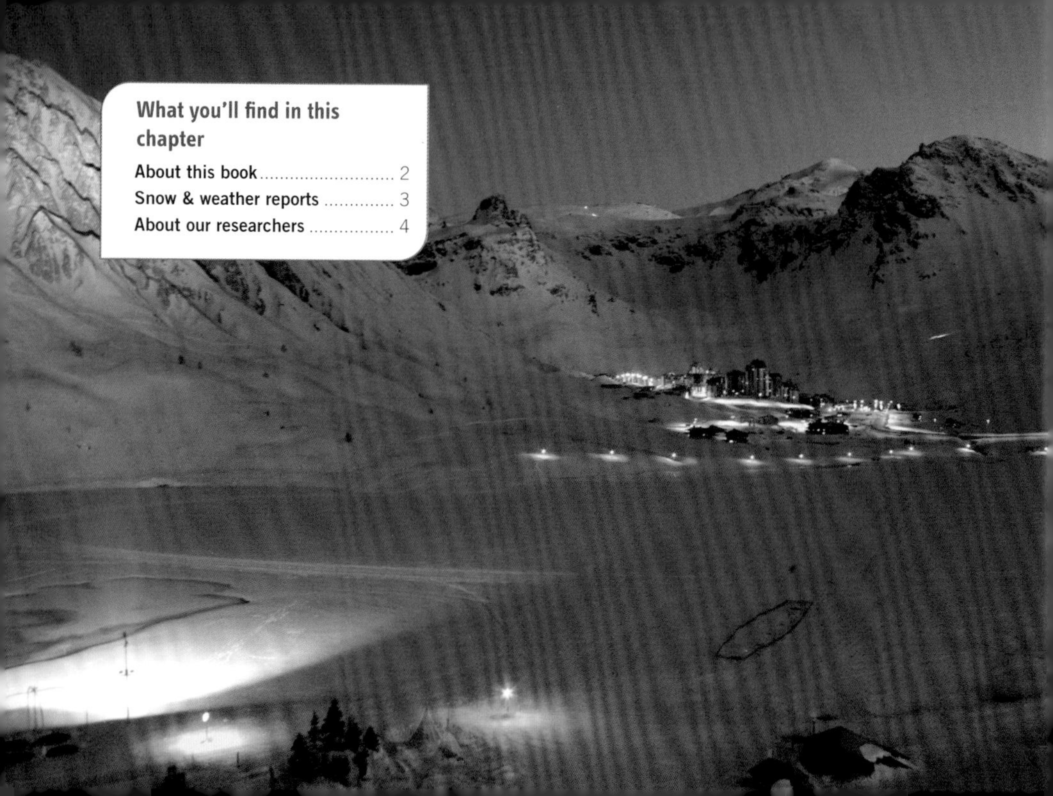

What you'll find in this chapter

About Mad Dog Ski

My time in the mountains used to be restricted to one or two precious weeks a year. Each winter, I would arrive with my ski buddies, eager to get on the slopes as soon as possible, indulge in some good après-ski and ensure we had somewhere decent to re-fuel at lunchtimes. All too often, this precious information comes the day before you're heading home.

During my first season as a thirty-something chalet host, I realised I wasn't alone in my quest for reliable information. Week after week guests would ask the same questions; where should they ski, where were the best places to eat and drink, the best mountain restaurant, how do you get there? Mad Dog Ski was born.

Everything in our books and on maddogski.com is researched by skiers and boarders who know the resort they are writing about inside out.

Not only that, but we are passionate about helping our readers get the most out of their holiday from the moment they arrive to the moment they leave. We want you to love the resort and the mountains as much as we do.

With Mad Dog Ski, we always give you our independent view – extra special places and people are shown throughout this book as 'Mad Dog favourites'. If our taste varies from yours, or if you find places we haven't, please write to us or email us at **info@maddogski.com.**

Enjoy the mountain!
Kate Whittaker
Founder, Mad Dog Ski

About this book

Mad Dog books are designed to be most use when you actually get to Tignes. To keep them small enough for your ski jacket pocket, we've stuck to just the essentials. For the full lowdown on planning your trip (your travel options, where to stay and that kind of thing) check out **maddogski.com**. If you can't find what you're looking for or have a particularly tricky question, check out the Ask Mad Dog area at the bottom of the homepage where you can email us – we love a challenge!

We're not perfect!

Whilst we make every effort to get things right, places, prices and opening times do change from season to season. If you spot an error or if you simply have a different opinion to us, get in contact at **info@maddogski.com**.

Prices

All prices are based on the 2006/7 season. Prices for food, drink and services in resort are given in euros (€).

Skier or boarder?

Throughout this book, 'skiing' and 'skier' are used as interchangeable terms for 'riding' and 'snowboarder'. No offence is intended – it just helps make our books smaller.

Telephone numbers

All numbers are prefixed by their French dialling code. Landlines in Tignes are prefixed by the code '04 79' (so +33 (0)4 79…) whilst French mobiles start with an '06' (+33 (0)6…).

To call France from the UK, dial '+33' and drop the first '0' of the French number. From France to the UK, dial '+44' and omit the first '0' of the UK number.

Public telephones that accept phone cards (available from Tabacs > 101) are available throughout resort. If you plan to use your UK mobile in Tignes, you'll need to enable it for international roaming before leaving the UK. You pay to receive calls as well as to make them, so text messages are often a cheaper way to stay in touch.

Snow and weather reports

For up-to-date information about the resort, **maddogski.com** has snow reports, weather forecasts and webcams for Tignes.

You can also sign up for our regular newsletter.

Tell us what you think!

Tell us about your favourite (or least favourite) places in Tignes at maddogski.com. Simply check out the entry under Tignes and 'Add your review'.

Home
Guidebooks
Features
News
Ski weekends
Gallery
Get in touch

Resorts
Austria
France
Switzerland

SIGN UP & WIN

Tignes - France

The French ski resort of Tignes is located in the Haute Tarentaise of the Savoie region of France. Famed for its extensive ski area, off-piste terrain and popularity with hardcore skiers and snowboarders, Tignes has some of the most snow-sure skiing in the region.

Tignes ("Teen") is unfairly renowned for being the ugly resort in the Espace Killy, and indeed, if it's a chocolate box Alpine experience you're after, then stay elsewhere. But if you want a snow sure resort with a huge variation of fantastic skiing, then Tignes does not disappoint.

Tucked into a hanging valley in the Haute Tarentaise, Tignes has five villages, 300km of varied pistes, a glacier and access to a huge amount of breathtaking back country riding through the Vanoise National Park. Whilst the nightlife is not on the level of Verbier or neighbouring Val d'Isere, Tignes seems to have the right balance of apres-ski and sport. Our Where to stay section has more...

Key info

Resort altitude	1550m - 2100m
Highest lift	3455m
Lowest lift	1550m
Kms of piste	300kms
No of lifts	90
Black pistes	12%
Red pistes	27%
Blue pistes	46%
Green pistes	15%
Snow parks	2
Glacier	Yes
Snowmaking	635

Morzine
Le Grand Bornand
Magève
Chamonix
Sainte Foy
Les Arcs
La Plagne
Tignes
Courchevel
Val d'Isere
Meribel
Les Deux-Alpes
Serre Chevalier

Tignes guidebook

Buy now

More...
Where to stay
Planning your trip
On the piste
Food and drink
Other activities
Families
The list
Webcams and weather

Snow reports

Tignes
Report date: 27 Nov 2007
Last snowed: 15 Nov 2007
Fresh snow! 10cm
Lifts open: 30 out of 47

Snow depth
Lower slopes: 30cm
Upper slopes: 50cm

Piste information
On-piste: Hard
Off-piste: Varied
Resort runs: Closed

3

About our researchers

Gaby de Pace

Gaby researched the Tignes guide after three winter and two summer seasons snowboarding and working in the resort. Jobs in the resort involved running the Tignes Scene newspaper with pro-skier James Vernon, working as a resort manager, a waitress and last and most definitely the least favourite, working 20 hour days as a transfer rep for a tour operator.

Favourite restaurant: Le Caveau, with friends > 66
Best après-ski: A sunny afternoon on any terrace, drinking until the sun drops behind the mountains
Favourite mountain restaurant: L'Arolay in Le Fornet, Val d'Isère – rustic, warming food with very French service > 90
Best run: The off-piste from the Col Pers

Alistair Emmet

A keen all-round mountain man, Alistair spends as much free time as possible snowboarding, skiing, hiking and climbing. After having owned and run the Loop Bar in Le Lac for four years, he now goes out to Tignes as much as possible to get fresh lines. He has helped write and research many of the entries in this guide.

Favourite restaurant: Dinner with friends at the Clin d'Oeil > 69
Best après-ski: TC's Bar in Lavachet for a friendly place to drink > 80
Favourite lunch stop: L'Armailly in Les Brévières – satisfying after a run through the trees > 71
Best run: Anything off-piste on the north face of the Pramecou

Tignes; the insider's guide to what makes it the resort of choice for so many serious skiers and boarders.

What you'll find in this chapter

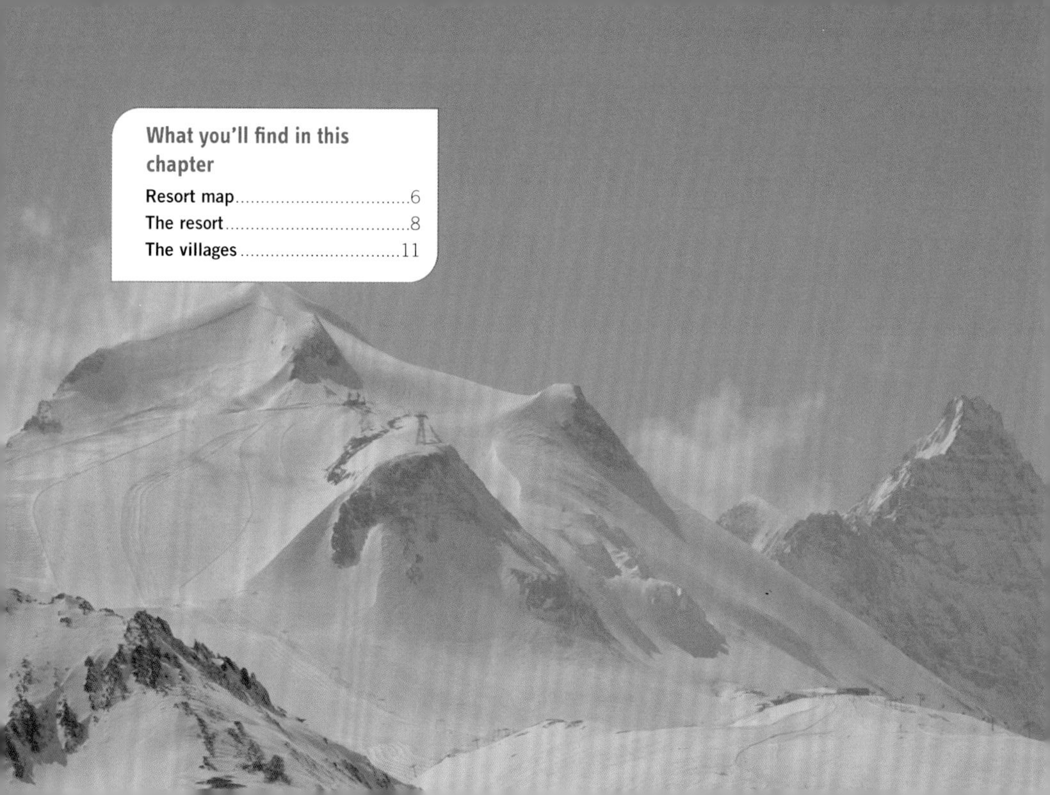

Tucked into a hanging valley in the Haute Tarentaise, Tignes has five villages, 300km of varied pistes, a glacier and access to a huge amount of breathtaking back country riding through the Vanoise National Park.

Whilst the nightlife is not on the level of Verbier or neighbouring Val d'Isère, Tignes seems to have the right balance of après-ski and sport. And, if it's off the slopes activities you're interested in, the resort has plenty to offer non-skiers, thrill seekers and families alike.

Tignes is unfairly renowned for being the ugly resort in the Espace Killy, and indeed, if it's a chocolate box Alpine experience you're after, stay elsewhere. But if you want a snow-sure resort with a huge variation of fantastic skiing, Tignes does not disappoint.

Tignes at a glance

- Around 30,000 beds to fill
- Only 53% of visitors are from outside France
- 300km of pistes across the Espace Killy
- 1900m vertical drop from the Grande Motte glacier (3456m) down to Les Brévières (1550m)

There is a reason after all, why many of Europe's professional riders choose Tignes as their home each winter.

Tignes' villages

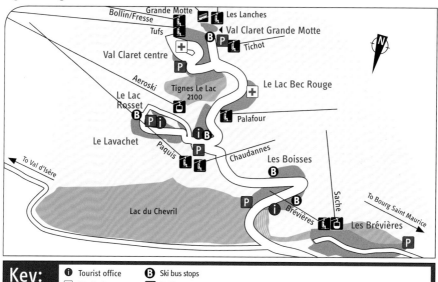

Key:

- ℹ Tourist office
- ✚ Medical centre
- Ⓑ Ski bus stops
- 🅿 Parking

The resort

Tignes is made up of five villages; three of them clustered around a frozen lake in an upper valley. Altitudes range from 1550m to 2300m. Each offers something different, making it easy to find the atmosphere you are looking for. From traditional wooden chalets to basic apartment blocks to decadent hotels, there is accommodation for most tastes and budgets. Most of the villages are self-contained with their own restaurants, bars and shops but if you want to travel around, free buses connect four of the villages, making getting around easy.

So, where to stay out of Tignes' five villages? The highest villages, Val Claret, Le Lac and Le Lavachet

---

Orientation: Tignes' main landmarks and areas

Village maps on > 124.

Val Claret

Val Claret centre: the main part of the village including the road and pedestrian centre.

Grande Motte: the lower part of the village including the main lift departure point.

Le Lac

Rue de la Poste: the road that runs from the Maison de Tignes up the hill past the Post Office.

Maison de Tignes: the huge wooden building in the centre of Le Lac with a pisted area one side and a bus station on the lower side.

Le Rosset: the road that runs alongside the nursery slope.

---

at around 2100m, are bigger and have direct access to snow-sure pistes and therefore tend to be more popular. However Les Boisses and Les Brévières lower down the valley have their own distinct charm and prices are cheaper.

Whilst all the villages have ski in, ski out accommodation and beginner slopes nearby, the ski schools tend to meet in Val Claret, Le Lac and Les Brévières.

Still waters...

As you drive to Tignes, it's difficult not to notice the huge lake (Lac du Chevril) and barrage (dam) that you cross to reach the higher villages of the ski resort. However, many visitors remain unaware that underneath the calm and often frozen surface of the lake lies the original village of Tignes.

Just after WW II, a small picturesque farming village sat by the side of the Isère river. The new sport of skiing was beginning to grow in popularity and skiers were starting to visit the village and neighbouring Val d'Isère. In 1946, the Tignes residents were shocked to discover that the Government had decided to build a dam on their section of the river in order to generate electricity.

In 1952, after a long and bitter struggle, the residents were turned out of their homes and the dam was finally constructed. Whilst most families chose to move away, a few decided to try their luck with the compensation land that had been offered higher up in the mountains.

Just a few years later, in 1957, the first ski-season opened at 2100m and because of its height and abundance of snow, Tignes soon became a popular resort. The original families that took a chance on the new Tignes still own much of the land as well as many of the hotels, restaurants and ski schools happily justifying their brave move.

The villages

Val Claret (2300m)

The highest village of the resort is Val Claret at 2300m and with this elevated status comes a wealth of shops, restaurants and bars. Nightlife here is the best in Tignes with two popular nightclubs just 200 metres from each other. Set over two levels, the main hub of the village is on the upper level while the ski lifts, main car park and bus route are on the lower level. Take one of the two lifts either end to get between levels or ski down.

Val Claret has brilliant ski access with direct links to the Espace Killy, the Grande Motte glacier and the Tignes bowl. Its proximity to the glacier means it's the only village with direct access to summer and winter skiing. Most of the lifts here have been recently modernised to make them faster and more comfortable.

Le Lac (2100m)

Le Lac gives Val Claret a run for its money in the popularity stakes with just as many amenities, spread over two areas: Rue de la Poste and Le Rosset. With the wooden Maison de Tignes tourist office as its centrepiece, this village is usually the place where resort events are held.

Access to the ski area is also good, with the Aeroski, a fast gondola, providing quicker access to the Espace Killy than the Val Claret lifts. Home of **Trolles**, the thrill-seeker's black run, Le Lac also boasts some great blue runs down to resort from the top of the newly replaced Palafour lift; ideal for beginners just off the nursery slopes.

Le Lavachet

Home of self-catering apartments and also of many season workers, Lavachet is located just behind Le Rosset in Le Lac. Despite being so close to Le Lac, it does possess its own sense of community and has a supermarket as well as several bars and restaurants.

Two chairlifts operate out of the lower part of the village: Paquis which takes you to the Espace Killy and Chaudannes which provides access to Les Brévières.

The free Lavachet nursery slope has a drag lift which also provides skiing access to the Le Lac nursery slope.

Les Boisses (1850)

Situated on the road up to the main parts of Tignes, Les Boisses is the quietest village with just a couple of bars and restaurants – most of them located in hotels.

Les Boisses offers some of the best value accommodation in the resort and is also great for securing tricky weekend bookings. If it all gets too quiet for you in the evenings, get the free bus (> 113) up to the higher villages or a taxi down to Les Brévières.

Les Boisses has direct access to the slopes to get to the rest of the ski area, and its altitude means it is as snow-sure as many nearby resorts. A new four-man chairlift for the 2007/8 season means access to the main ski area will be faster.

Les Brévières (1550)

If an authentic Alpine village is your cup of tea, then the lowest village of Les Brévières is your best choice. Ideal for families wanting a quiet (and often cheaper) break, Les Brévières has enough restaurants and bars to stop you missing the hustle and bustle of the higher villages. For those on a budget, there is also hostel-style accommodation > 18.

With a gondola taking you towards the Espace Killy, ski access is easy and varied for all levels of competence. The runs down to the village are shaded by trees making them perfect for white-out days or off-piste tree runs.

Don't leave Tignes without...

- Lunching at the Folie Douce followed by dancing on tables ➤ 87

- Skidooing around the mountains at dusk, stopping for a welcome vin chaud along the way ➤ 96

- Shopping for local produce from the Savoyard La Grange shop in Val Claret ➤ 101

- Visiting the SPOT area for some realistic lessons in off-piste rescue ➤ 32

- Skiing off the side of a mountain and floating down to reality on a paraglider ➤ 98

Independent ski and snowboard company, run by three friends who know just about everyone you'll need during your stay in Tignes.

We put together tailor-made holidays to suit all our customers' needs:
Over 20 apartments and chalets to chose from
Catered or self-catered accommodation

Our friendly and reliable staff can help you with:
Transfers to and from the resort
Ski and board rental
Organising lessons and guides

We give you everything you could wish for on an independent holiday – at an affordable price!

You can ring us in Tignes on +33 (0)627 877188
or in the UK on +44 (0)771 2761925 and +44(0)207 2320086
www.flatline-tignes.com • www.TignesSpirit.com

Helping you to
plan your trip;
your travel options,
where to stay and
useful tips.

Our books are designed to be a handy companion in resort. To keep them pocket-sized, we put the reams of planning information and tips on our website **maddogski.com**. This chapter gives you a simple overview together with useful websites and contacts.

maddogski.com

- Travel advice, including getting to France (self-drive, trains, airlines and ferries) and how to get to resort once you arrive (airport transfers, car hire and buses)
- Accommodation, including reviews of chalets, hotels and apartments
- Everything else you need to know before you book your trip, from winter sports insurance to the latest snow reports

Getting there

The closest airport to Tignes is Chambéry – the capital of the Savoie region – although only a few airlines fly there whereas the larger airports of Geneva and Lyon St Exupéry get the majority of ski routes and have the most flexible flight times. Ryanair's recent addition of Grenoble to its timetable is a good option for a cheap flight and shorter transfer time.

The snow trains run by Rail Europe and Eurostar are a more eco-friendly route to the Alps and whilst pricier than low-cost airlines, the journey is relaxing. The nearest train station to Tignes is in Bourg Saint Maurice (about 30km away). Whilst the sleeper train makes the most out of your time, beware that you get into resort early morning and accommodation is often not ready this early. Use the showers and baggage drop in the Maison de Tignes offices (> 123).

To get from the airport or the train station to Tignes, public buses (> 20) run from the major airports (Chambéry, Geneva and Lyon St Exupéry) through Bourg and up to Tignes regularly. Expect to pay from €50 for a round trip.

For door-to-door service, private transfers and taxis are the best option, especially if there are a group of you. There are also a number of English-speaking transfer companies that operate out of resort who are good for both price and reliability – very useful too if you have an early morning flight!

Driving from the UK, it should take about 11 hours to drive from Calais. It will cost around €50-60 in toll fees which you can pay in cash or by UK credit card (not debit card).

Airport transfer times

Airport	Airlines	km to Tignes	Approx. transfer time by road
Chambéry	Flybe, Flyglobespan, Jet2	142km	2 hours
Geneva	Air France, bmi baby, BA, easyJet, Flybe, Flyglobespan, Jet 2	200km	3 hours
Grenoble	BA, easyJet, Ryanair, Thomsonfly	210km	2.5 hours
Lyon St Exupéry	Air France, bmi baby, BA, easyJet	220km	2.5 hours

fast track to tignes with the snow train

Why not take the Rail Europe's Snow Train? Depart Friday night from either St Pancras or Ebbsfleet International on Eurostar and connect with the overnight service in Paris. You'll arrive fresh for a full day of skiing on Saturday morning. Return the following Saturday night.

- **Enjoy 2 extra days on the slopes!**
- **Comfortable, flat-bed sleeping accommodation**
- **Stops at 6 stations serving 25 resorts**
- **Bar and disco carriages**
- **Skis and snowboards go free**
- **Short, easy transfers to resort**
- **Bi-lingual reps on board**

return from

£219

for Tignes take the Snow Train to Bourg St Maurice

for more information and to book
call **0844 848 4062** or visit www.raileurope.co.uk

RAIL EUROPE

Where to stay

Although in recent years the selection of hotels and chalets in Tignes has improved, the mainstay of accommodation is still self-catered apartments. Recent developments have all been built in traditional Alpine style, softening the austerity of the apartment blocks and creating a bigger choice of luxury accommodation.

The **About Tignes** (➤ 5) chapter gives the characters and facilities for the different villages. One of the plus points about the resort is that nowhere is far from the slopes and the free bus service will get you around easily.

For those who want to stay in style as well as comfort, try one of the new residences in Val Claret,

CHG (cgh-residences.com) which offer spacious luxury apartments. Alternatively, the **Village Montana** in Le Lac has both apartments and hotel rooms popular with UK guests. Mid-priced independent hotels that are worth checking out include the **Hotel Diva** (hoteldiva-tignes. com) in Val Claret for a good hotel for families. **The Alpaka** (alpaka. com) in Le Lac is a British run hotel with a lively bar and the nearby **Campanules** (campanules.com), is a luxury option.

Tignes has recently seen a number of traditional ski chalets being built and now many of the newer luxury ones are on tour operators' books. There are however, a number of independent chalets that cater for specific

markets. **The Dragon Lodge** (dragonlodge.com) runs a chilled chalet for snowboarders, **Chalet Chardons** (chaletchardons.com) in Les Brévières is the place to go for budget conscious backpackers or single travellers. **Le Dome** (ledome. co.uk) in Les Boisses specialises in short breaks and offers a good value flexible option.

If you're after self-catering apartments, you'll be spoilt for choice. As well as the huge number on offer on the central **Tignes Reservations** website (tignesreservation.net), there is also the British run **Tignes.co.uk** (tignes.co.uk) and **FlatLine Tignes** (flatline-tignes.com) who both rent out a range of apartments.

Useful numbers and websites

Airports

Chambéry
T +33 (0)4 79 54 43 54
W chambery.aeroport.fr

Grenoble
T +33 (0)4 76 65 48 48
W grenoble.aeroport.fr

Geneva
T +41 (0)22 717 71 11
W gva.ch

Lyon St Exupéry
T +33 (0)4 26 00 70 07
W lyonairport.com

Airlines

Air France
T +44 (0)870 142 4343
W airfrance.co.uk

British Airways
T +44 (0)870 850 9850
W britishairways.com

bmi baby
T +44 (0)871 224 0224
W bmibaby.com

easyJet
T +44 (0)905 821 0905
W easyjet.com

Flybe
T +44 (0)871 522 6100
W flybe.com

Jet2
T +44 (0)871 226 1737
W jet2.com

Thomsonfly
T +44 (0)870 165 0079
W thomsonfly.com
Doncaster flights to Geneva

Trains

Eurostar
T +44 (0)870 518 6186
W eurostar.com

Rail Europe
T +44 (0)8708 371 371
W raileurope.co.uk

SNCF
T +33 (0) 892 35 35 35
W voyages-sncf.com

Buses

Altibus
T +33 (0)4 79 68 32 96
W altibus.com
Buses from Chambéry, Geneva
and Bourg Saint Maurice

Satobus
T +33 (0)4 27 00 70 07
W satobus-alps.com
Buses from Lyon St Exupéry

Car hire

Auto Europe
T +44 (0)800 358 1229
W auto-europe.co.uk

Avis
T +44 (0)844 581 0147
W avis.co.uk

easyCar
T +44 (0)8710 500 444
W easycar.co.uk

Europcar
T +44 (0)870 607 5000
W europcar.co.uk

Hertz
T +44 (0)870 844 8844
W hertz.co.uk

For details of parking and garages
in Tignes > 113.

Private transfers
The Cool Bus
T +33 (0)6 32 19 29 62
W thecoolbus.co.uk

Snowstar Holidays
T +44 (0)870 068 6611
W snowstarholidays.com

Tignes.co.uk
W tignes.co.uk
Bookings online only

Taxis
Anenome Taxis
T +33 (0)6 09 41 01 46
W taxitignes.com

Diane Taxis
T +33 (0)4 79 06 30 32

Taxis Regine
T +33 (0)4 79 06 36 43
W taxis2savoie.com

Self-drive advice
Via Michelin route planner
W viamichelin.co.uk

Driving abroad advice
W drivingabroad.co.uk

Ferries
Brittany Ferries
T +44 (0)870 366 5333
W brittany-ferries.com
From Poole, Portsmouth
and Plymouth

P&O
T +44 (0)870 598 03 33
W poferries.com
From Dover and Portsmouth

Seafrance
T +44 (0)870 571 17 11
W seafrance.com
From Dover to Calais

Alternatively **ferrybooker.com** and
cheap4ferries.com offer a selection
of fares from various companies.

Insurance
Snowcard
T +441327 262805
W snowcard.co.uk

Ski Club of Great Britain
T +44 (0)845 601 94227
W skiclubinsurance.co.uk

Ski Insurance
T +44 (0)870 755 6101
W ski-insurance.co.uk

You can also buy insurance with
your lift pass ('carré neige'– €2.50
per day) which covers you for
recovery from the mountain
without having to prove you're

insured or paying up front (should you be unfortunate enough to need it).

Lift passes
If you're very organised, you can buy your lift passes online (> 35).

Families
Travelling with children? We recommend booking childcare (> 106) before you arrive.

Tourist office
T +33 4 79 40 04 40
W tignes.net (> 125).

Mobile Board Rental

Remove all the hassle from your snowboard hire.

Top end equipment delivered directly to your door at extremely competitive prices.

Whatever your level of snowboarding experience, get fitted out by our staff with the latest technology in boards, boots and bindings, all in the comfort of your holiday accomodation.

Take a look at our website for all this year's equipment and prices to hire or buy.

With a free collection service at the end of your stay, why battle the crowds at the rental shop?

Book in advance or in resort. Call us in Tignes on +33 (0) 627 877188

www.TignesBoardRental.com

or email info@flatline-tignes.com

In partnership with Noble Custom, Option Snowboards, NFA, Endeavor, SP and Ortovox

photographer: Véremie Pontin

This chapter gets you **on the piste** and around the mountain as quickly as possible – after all it's why you're here.

What you'll find in this chapter

Tignes sits on the side of one of the most varied and expansive ski areas in the world. Whether it's back country powder, technical mogul runs, snowparks or just mile upon mile of cruisy blue runs, it has enough to keep every standard of skier busy.

The ski area

A recent ski lift modernisation programme has seen many of the lifts in the Tignes valley rebuilt to be faster and more comfortable meaning that many of the long queues have disappeared and getting around is a lot faster. A hands-free electronic pass system has also been introduced – streamlining the process of getting onto the lifts. With all the runs back into resort serviced by snow cannons, even in snow sparse years, it is possible to ski all the way back to resort.

Grande Motte glacier

Tignes' famous glacier is one of the must-see experiences of your week. Standing at 3656m, the glacier can be in bright sunshine when the rest of the resort is in cloud. That said, it is also the first to close in bad weather. For quick access take the funicular up to the Panoramic restaurant (> 85), or for better views, take the sunny Les Lanches chair followed by the Vanoise Express. Then catch the cable car up to the very top for views that take in Mont Blanc as well as the neighbouring Italian peaks.

Beginners should head back down in the cable car whilst intermediates and above can look forward to one of the longest runs in the ski area – a leg burning 1556m descent. Charge from the top of **Glacier** or **Descente**, all the way back down to Val Claret, popping into the snowpark on your way into resort.

Les Brévières

This makes for the perfect day out, especially if you are in a mixed ability group. Various ability pistes wind their way down through the

Les Brévières trees with some picturesque photo opportunities along the way. Beginners and those looking for a relaxing run should head down **Rhodedendron/Mélèzes/Myrtilles** from the top of the Chaudannes chairlift. Intermediates can branch off onto **Chardons/Pavot** halfway down the blue runs. And for the ultimate black run experience, take the mogul-laden **Sache** run all the way down from the top of the L'Aiguille Percée. Reward yourself at the bottom with an indulgent lunch at L'Etoile des Neiges or L'Armailly restaurant (> 71).

Tignes bowl

The Tignes valley lends itself naturally to a great circuit of easy confidence boosting, leg warming runs. For more advanced riders, there's also a wealth of off-the-sides off-piste and tons of hits for jibbing. Start at whatever point is closest to you and try and take in as many highlights as possible.

The Palafour lift from Le Lac serves the popular **Anemone** or **Lys** runs which are cruisy enough for early beginners but also have lots of hits for playing around on. Alternatively, head up to L'Aiguille Percée (eye of the needle) – a group of jagged peaks overlooking Le Lac. Go to the eye to get some great views and maybe stop for a picnic before taking the choice of blacks, reds and blues down from here.

Take Tichot followed by Grattalu chairlifts for access to some fun intermediate runs. For an off-piste learning experience, head to the SPOT hut at the bottom of the Grattalu chair to learn about off-piste safety and rescue techniques (> 32). If it's open, head up the Col des Ves for some controlled off-piste runs.

Tovière

You can't miss this mountain with its dramatic craggy face next to the frozen lake. Reach the top by the Le Lac Aeroski or Val Claret's Tufs chairlift. From here you can access the main ski area between Tignes and Val d'Isère. The array of different runs offer something for everyone. Take **Creux** and then

progression ki nowboard school

Leading British Ski School, Val d'Isere-Tignes-Ste Foy

Skiing Snowboarding Telemark

- Brilliant & Safe Kids Group Lessons
- High End Clinics (Mini Groups)
- Small Group lessons
- Private Lessons to suit
- Cool Teen Clinics
- Superb Off Piste

Progression Ski and Snowboard donate 1% of turnover to environmental charities and foundations.

www.progressionski.com
tel 0208 123 3001   enquiries@progressionski.com

Verte down to La Daille in Val d'Isère or jump on the Mont Blanc lift and head to the snowpark (➤ 30). Beginners should go to the **Grande Pré** for an easy circuit where they can practise their turns or advanced skiers can try out their skills on the legendary Olympic **Face** (➤ 51). All routes down in this area take you to Val d'Isère so make sure you catch the Tommeuses lift back to Tignes before it closes – or face a €40 taxi ride back there.

Val d'Isère

Popping over to Val d'Isère on skis is a lot easier than on the road and it is well worth a visit, as are its slopes. Make a full day out of it by visiting Le Fornet or head over for a short visit to the Solaise area.

Whilst it is possible to ski all the way over to both, beginners might want to ski to La Daille and get the free ski bus as some of the connecting runs can be quite mogulled.

Solaise is a nice sunny area to go as an early intermediate, as the runs are wide and easy. Intermediates can try one of the runs over towards the Le Fornet – the pipe-like **Piste 'L'** and the road run **Germain Mattis** are both fun runs with varying gradients. Off-piste skiers may want to head to the back of Solaise where the recently replaced Cugnai lift serves the Manchet Valley. For those who love their off-piste tree skiing, the Mattis trees from

the above red run are steep and deep after snowfall.

Le Fornet, the furthest of the ski area from Tignes, is perfect for a full day out when your legs are ready. Often the forgotten area, it is normally fairly quiet and the powder here is the last to get tracked out. For an exciting journey there, take the Leissieres Express from the Solaise area – locally known as the 'up and over', it's worth a go. Along with a glacier, Le Fornet has lots of wide blue runs, some serious trees and also provides access to some fantastic off-piste/touring routes over into the next valley.

Beginners

Beginners in Tignes might be concerned about the lack of green runs. However, many of the blues in the ski area are as wide and easy as a green so don't be put off by them. There are also are five nursery slopes in Tignes (marked on the piste map in a red and yellow dotted line) all of which are free to ski on. Both Le Lac's Rosset and Val Claret's Bollin slopes are the best as they are served by chairlifts, although they can get busy with lessons. The Bollin slope is slightly harder as it gets quite steep and is also a through route from the mountains above so it gets busy with different levels of skier. There are drag lift served slopes in Val Claret centre, Le Lavachet and down in Les Brévières.

As these slopes are free, you don't need to buy a lift pass until you want to progress onto the greens and blues on offer.

Boarders

Tignes is very popular with snowboarders and the majority of its runs and lifts have been designed with boarders in mind. With the exception of some of the nursery slopes and a few advanced areas, it is possible to never need to take a drag lift. Equally, there aren't that many areas that are so flat that snowboarders will need to get off and walk. The runs to keep a lot of speed up on are **Génépy** down from the Grande Motte, **Myrtilles** down to Les Brévières and **Cognon** in Le Fornet.

Freestylers have the choice of two snowparks (> 30) as well as plenty of runs with ledges, hits and natural kickers all over the ski area. The park scene in Tignes is big and there are always people around to hook up with to practise tricks.

Freeriders have an amazing amount of terrain to explore from gentle powder fields such as the tongue of the Grande Motte to steep and narrow couloirs lining the faces of mountains such as Pramecou and Chardonnet. For more detail on off-piste in Tignes see > 32 and for a new mobile snowboard hire service in the resort, see > 42.

Snowparks

There are two snowparks in the Espace Killy but the Val d'Isère park is much bigger and better maintained than the Tignes park. Located underneath the Mont Blanc chair, it has different gradients of kickers, rails and boxes as well as a sound system and T-bar. There is normally a vibrant atmosphere up here and it's well worth spending some time practising new tricks.

The Tignes park is situated near the bottom of **Double 'M'** and whilst not being big or snow-sure, it does normally have two pipes – a super pipe and a learning pipe. There are quite often competitions happening here.

Off-piste

The Espace Killy has some of the best and most varied off-piste skiing in the Alps. Because of this, Tignes sets aside a section of the ski area to teach people about off-piste. The SPOT area, at the bottom of the Grattalu chair above Val Claret, offers free advice about rescue techniques, which areas are unsafe, as well as a controlled off-piste area on the side of Pramecou. Drop by if you're going off-piste – the idea is to educate rather than to admonish so it's worth being honest about where you want to ski.

If you're interested in going off-piste but don't know the area, it is always best to take a guide with you. Tignes unfortunately has had a high number of off-piste deaths in the last few years – mainly due to skiers not knowing the terrain and being unequipped to deal with accidents and avalanches. To read more on the subject, the **Pistehors** website (pistehors.com) offers up-to-date advice and information about off-piste skiing in Tignes.

With a guide you can explore all the secret spots and discover parts of mountains that are full of local wildlife and amazing scenery. The Vanoise National park sits behind the Espace Killy and is an ideal place for touring or back country skiing. The company opposite specialises in off-piste guiding but many of the ski schools offer guiding as well (➤ 37).

Heli-skiing in banned in France but you can ski just over the border in Italy. Most ski schools (> 37) can organise this for you.

Bureau des Guides
T +33 (0)4 79 06 42 76
W guidesdetignes.com.
Le *Nevada in Val Claret and in Richermoz sports in Le Lac Rosset*. Off-piste guiding and ski touring.

Avalanche!

Whilst Tignes' piste security works extremely hard to prevent avalanches, the danger cannot be completely averted and every year people do die on the mountain.

Speed is of the essence if you are caught in an avalanche; if the victim is alive after the initial impact there is an 80% chance of survival if rescued in the first 12 minutes, after 15 minutes the probability of a successful rescue drops dramatically. Your best chance of survival is to be rescued by someone in your own group; a transceiver, shovel and probe are essential kit for off-piste skiing.

Although manufacturers claim that mobile phones cause minimum interference with transceiver signals, it is also recommended that you switch your mobile off whilst off-piste.

The avalanche risk is shown clearly with flags and avalanche ratings (on a scale of 1-5) throughout the Espace Killy. If in doubt, visit the SPOT zone (> 30) for some free advice and training or ask a piste security (dressed in black and yellow).

Piste security
Tignes: +33 (0)4 79 06 32 00
Val d'Isère:
+33 (0)4 79 06 02 10

Avalanche warning flags

Yellow
Limited risk

|3-4|

Black/yellow chequered flag
High risk

5

Black flag
Very high risk

Cross-country

There are two cross-country skiing areas in Tignes; around the lake and on the glacier, but as they aren't marked on the piste map you'll need to pick up a separate map and details from the tourist office (> 123).

Alternatively hire a guide (> 30) and explore the territory around the Espace Killy and the Vanoise National Park.

Lift passes

Lift passes in the Espace Killy are now electronic cards that you place in your left-hand jacket pocket (away from your mobile phone and anything metal) to operate the turnstiles as you pass through them.

Three different types of pass:

The EcoPass
Hands-free card access to the ski area.

The Liber'Tignes
Rechargeable card (€3) that you can top up online (**ski-tignes.com**) or at a ticket office for up to three years.

The VIP Pass'Tignes
Reserved for regular clients, this card costs €10 and can be recharged as above. Holders can also benefit from numerous discounts and offers.

If you're organised, you can book your ski pass online at **ski-tignes.com** and get the passes sent to your home.

Lift pass tips

- You now only need photos for passes of eight days or more, children under five years and seniors over 75 years
- The EcoPass is recyclable – look out for the card bins at the lift pass offices
- The Liber'Tignes cards require a photo
- Children passes are from 5–12 years, teenagers from 13-17 years inclusive – see > 108 for details of prices and family packages
- Senior passes are for 60-74 years inclusive
- Children under five and seniors over 75 ski for free

Adult lift pass prices 2006/7
(Espace Killy and with carre neige insurance)

No. of days	Adult	Senior
Half day	€32.50	€27.50
1	€43.50	€37.00
6	€212.50	€180.00
7	€243.50	€206.00
10	€303.50	€257.00
14	€373.50	€317.00
Season	€957.00	€813.50

For details of children passes and family discounts, see > 108.

Lift pass offices
STGM main office
T +33 (0)4 79 06 60 12
W ski-tignes.com
Val Claret, Grande Motte, 8am-5pm (7pm Saturdays).
There are also lift pass kiosks at all of the Maison de Tignes offices around the resort, some of them with lift pass vending machine.

Lost passes
Keep hold of your receipt and if you lose your pass, take it to the closest lift pass office with some ID. A duplicate of your ski pass valid from the following day will be issued. A small processing fee will be charged.

Lift closing times

Opening and closing times vary throughout the season so it is worth checking what time the last lift is if you're venturing further afield. The times can be found on the back of the piste map or at the lift stations themselves.

Piste accidents

In the case of an accident on the slopes or off-piste, call piste security on:

Tignes +33 (0)4 79 06 32 00
Val d'Isère +33 (0)4 79 06 02 10

Remember to give the operator detailed information on the location of the accident and the number of causalities. If you have some idea of the injuries sustained then let them know that too. If on a piste, it is a good idea to stand your skis or board in the snow above the victim to warn people coming down the hill.

Safety

Travelling at high speed is one of the great attractions of skiing but with it comes an element of danger.

Most accidents are caused by collisions; it is relatively easy for adult skiers to achieve speeds of over 50kph, even children can quite easily reach 45kph. Be aware of others and make sure you follow the piste rules.

Rules of the piste

1. Respect – do not endanger or prejudice the safety of others

2. Control – ski in control, adapting your speed and manner to ability, conditions and traffic. Give way to slower skiers

3. Choice of route – the uphill skier must choose his route so he does not endanger the skiers below

4. Overtaking – allowed left or right, above or below but always leave sufficient space for the overtaking skier

5. Entering and starting a run – look both up and down the piste before you head off

6. Stopping on the piste – avoid stopping at narrow or low visibility areas. Always stop at the edge of the piste rather than in the middle and make sure that you can be easily seen by approaching skiers

7. Climbing – if you have to walk up or down the piste, do so at the edge and ensure neither you nor your equipment are a danger to anyone else

8. Signs and markings – respect the information given about pistes and the weather

9. Accidents – if you witness an accident, you must give assistance, particularly by alerting piste security

10. Identification – if you are involved in or witness an accident, you must provide your identity to piste security if requested

The International Ski Federation (FIS) Code of Conduct

Weather

The weather can change rapidly in the mountains. Sunny weather can turn into cold low-visibility conditions in a matter of hours. If you can, check the weather reports posted at the base lift stations and in the tourist offices (> 123). Information boards at the bottom of the lifts also show which runs are open/closed, wind speed and the avalanche risk. Lift-operating staff can also give you information or you'll find weather reports on Tignes TV (> 122) or resort radio (> 121).

Bad weather days

There are often days when the wind is ripping around the mountains or it is snowing so hard that you can't see a thing. At these times, its best to ski in sheltered places such as the tree-lined runs down to Les Brévières or down to La Daille. When it's windy, the Grande Motte cable car is the first to close.

The tourist office publishes an event guide each week (*Animations*) that contains details of all activities put on during bad weather or look at **Other things to do** (> 93).

Ski and snowboard schools

As with most French ski resorts, the main ski school is the ubiquitous ESF (Ecole du Ski Français). However, in the last decade, there has been a rise in international schools such as Evolution 2 and latterly Progression and the all-snowboarding school, Alliance.

If you are holidaying at a peak period (school holidays, Christmas and New Year), it is worth booking your lessons as far in advance as possible as schools get booked up early. The prices we give here should be used as a guide only – check out the websites shown for up-to-date prices.

Alliance snowboarding school

T +33 (0)6 82 70 40 07
W alliancesnowboarding.com

Number of instructors: five
Private tuition: *€135 for two hours, €365 for full day (1/2 people)*
Group lessons: *€190 for five days (three hours per day)*
Max. group size: *six-eight*
Children: *same as above*
Set up in 2006, this very cool school is the only British snowboarding school in the Espace Killy. Easy to spot in their khaki green suits, they specialise in freestyle and freeriding and off-piste guiding. They also run pre-instructor training courses and special gap year training. As a small but very popular company, you'll need to book ahead to get with the Alliance.

ESF (Ecole du Ski Français)
Le Lac

T +33 (0)4 79 06 30 28
W esf-tignes.com
Next to Intersport at Palafour, 8.30am-6.30pm (7pm on weekends and Mondays).

Val Claret

T +33 (0)4 79 06 31 28
W esftignes.com
Val Claret centre, in new Le Nevada building.
Number of instructors: *250*
Private tuition: *from €91 for two hours, full day from €275 (price per instructor & up to five people)*
Group lessons: *€135 for six half days, €179 for five full days*
Max. group size: *12 for skiing, 10 for snowboarding*
Children: *lessons and a dedicated snow kindergarden (> 106)*
Two different ESFs operate out of Tignes and although you'd probably never tell the difference, they do have different contact details and meeting points. Being the largest ski school in Tignes, they have a wealth of instructors available making them flexible in terms of booking. Just make sure you request an English-speaking instructor. As well as the usual types of lessons (see below), they also run many other activities and the Le Lac branch has the only handicap skiing equipment in

the resort. Their latest products include ladies-only and senior ski days. Check out their ski show on a Monday night in Le Lac for some big air action.

Evolution 2

T +33 (0)4 79 06 35 76
W evolution2.com
Offices next Val Claret – next to Favre Sports in the centre and piste-side next to Le Coffee. Le Lac office by entrance to Palafour centre, 9am-12pm & 4-7-pm.
Number of instructors: *30*
Private tuition: *€50 for one hour (two people), €340 for full day of eight hours (up to four people)*
Group lessons: *eight (six for off-piste)*
Max. group size: *€180 for five lessons of three hours*

Children: *lessons and competitions (> 106)*
EV2 is one of the mainstays of the Tignes ski schools – with a number of offices across the resort, they are convenient to use. As well as private, specialist snowboard and technique group courses, they run some fantastic off-piste tours such as the Tarentaise tour that explores the Vanoise National Park (skiers only) or the exhilarating Tovière to Lac du Chevril descent.

Progression

T +44 (0)208 123 3001
W progressionski.com

Number of instructors: *10*
Private tuition: *€229 for three*

hours, €439 for all day*
Group lessons: *€270 for three hours for five days*
Max. group size: *eight for skiing, six for beginners*
Children: *group lessons and teenage clinics*
A fairly new school made up of long-time season workers and instructors from Val d'Isère. Expanding this year to include lessons in Tignes, Progression offers private and group lessons as well as general and technical clinics. They also teach telemarking, snowboarding and off-piste skills. And in an ethical move, they promise to donate 1% of their turnover to environmental schemes and charities.

Snocool

T +33 (0)4 79 24 30 94
W snocool.com
Le Lac, Rue de la Poste,
9am-12pm & 3-7.30pm.
Number of instructors: *eight*
Private tuition: *€45 for one hour,*
€320 for a full day
Group lessons: *€145 for three*
hours for five days
Max. group size: *six*
Children: *no specific children's*
lessons
Created in 1998 by a group of
French pro riders, this school has
been growing from strength to
strength. Positioning themselves
as freestyle and freeriding experts,
you are truly in the hands of riders
who have done it all and lived
in Tignes for a long time. Their
intimate knowledge of Tignes'
back country makes them a good
choice for guiding. You can also
get a discount on their rental
equipment when you book a
lesson with them.

Independent instructors
Skirevolution

T +33 (0)6 19 67 80 85
W skirevolution.com
Nick Quinn, a former training
executive for the British
Association of Snowsports
Instructors (BASI), is renowned for
his patient and thorough teaching
methods. Teaching skiing from
beginner level to race training to
BASI exam coaching, he is also
a good teacher for nervous and
unconfident skiers (> 43).

Equipment hire

Many of the hire shops offer very
similar equipment at comparable
prices. Your best bet is to
choose the outlet nearest to your
accommodation or use a shop that
will visit you at your chalet or hotel.
You are also more likely to get a
discount in the quieter mid-week.

If you've arranged a holiday
through a tour operator, many of
them offer discounts with the local
hire shops. If you know what you
want to hire, it's always best to
pre-book – almost all offer online
reservations. Most shops will offer
their own equipment insurance
– it's usually inexpensive and will
save you the hassle of paying
upfront should something happen
to your skis or board.

Black Cats

T +33 (0)4 79 06 42 46
W blackcats.fr
*Val Claret centre, 8.30am–
12.30pm & 3.30pm–7pm,
weekends: 8.30am-8pm.*
Specialist snowboard and freestyle
shop.

Flatline-Tignes: Board Rental

T +33 (0)6 27 87 71 88
W tignesboardrental.com
A new off-shoot to this apartment
website (> 18), Flatline-Tignes
Board Rental remove all the hassle
from hiring your snowboarding
equipment, providing good
quality kit directly to your door at
competitive prices. Whatever your
level of snowboarding experience,
they will fit you out with the latest
technology in boots, boards and
bindings, all in the comfort of your
holiday accommodation. The free
pick up service at the end of your
stay means you can avoid the
shop queues.

Precision

T +33 (0)4 79 06 46 93
W precision-ski.fr

*Le Lac Rosset, Monday to
Thursday: 8.30am-12.30pm &
3.30-7pm (from 2pm on Fridays),
Weekends: 8.30am-7.30pm.*
Large shop with clothes,
accessories and equipment to
sell or hire. To be picked up at
your accommodation, taken to
the hire shop and then dropped
back, call their mobile service on
+33 (0)6 99 81 33 14.

Snow Fun

W snowfun.com
*Eight shops all over resort: Hotel
le Diva, Palafour, Bec Rouge,
Curling, Brévières, Lavachet,
Chalet Club, Borsat, opening hours
vary – check website.*
With a shop almost always near
your accommodation, Snow Fun
mainly just deals in hire although
some shops sell equipment and
clothes. To be picked up at your
accommodation, taken to the hire
shop and then dropped back,
call their mobile service on
+33 (0)6 99 81 33 14.

TN'T

T +33 (0)8 99 70 07 69

Le Lac Rue de la Poste, 8.30am-7.30pm.
TN'T sells/hires hardware especially technical equipment such as off-piste, touring and climbing equipment. Niche equipment such as Never Summer snowboards are their speciality.

Piste rankings

It's a common scenario; poring over the piste map, trying to decide a plan for the day. You know the standard piste ranking system but, if you are just beginning to tackle reds, there's nothing worse than attempting a piste that is more black than red or tackling a black for the first time to find out that it is mogul hell. And more more experienced skiers looking for a specific challenge, the piste ranking system is too broad to be really useful. You can only have this in-depth knowledge if you live and ski all the pistes regularly.

Mad Dog Ski have teamed up with Nick Quinn from Skirevolution to rank the red and black pistes in the Espace Killy using a star rating (* = easier and *** = more challenging). Apart from the gradient and the width of the slope, we have also taken a number of other factors into account:

• North or south? North-facing slopes are more inclined to be icy, but keep the snow longer
• Traffic – less busy pistes can keep their snow longer but may not be pisted as often. Likewise very busy pistes can be hard to ski.
• Some pistes are groomed more frequently and some hardly ever
• Does the piste require a lot of snow to make it skiable?

About Nick Quinn

Nick runs a holiday rental company and ski school (skirevolution.com) in Tignes where he lives with his family. Previously he worked as a training executive for the British Association of Snowsports Instructors (BASI) in the Scottish resort of Aviemore. His skiing career began in the forces where he raced and taught for three years before becoming a fire-fighter for 13 years. These days, better known in Tignes for his patient and thorough teaching than his fire-fighting, he has provided us with his insights on the pistes in the Espace Killy ➤ 40.

Tignes red pistes

Piste	Comments	Connections
3500 **	Used primarily for race training in the summer and autumn.	3500
Ancolie *	Not too hard, Occasionally a few mogul sections.	Grand Huit
Bleuets *	Rolling and not too difficult until later in the season when it can get slushy.	Chaudannes
Chardons *	Rolling run, normally well-groomed, with some flatter sections.	Boisses
Colchiques **	Steep top and easy bottom and normally quiet.	Almes
Combe Folle *	Brilliant run kept in good condition that circuits the drag lift.	Combe Folle
Cretes **	Narrow, mogulled and icy at times although it opens up towards the bottom.	Tommeuses
Crocus *	Enjoyable rolling entry run to **Trolles**.	Paquis

Piste	Comments	Connections
Cyclamen **	Steep top section which can be rocky and icy when the snow is low. Otherwise easy.	Marais, Aiguille Percée
Dahu **	Flat at the top but a really nice steeper lower section which is often quiet.	Double Plan
Double 'M' *	A great quality red run but it can get quite busy.	Cairn
Face ***	Steep and narrow although short.	Grand Plan
Glacier **	A wide open run with some of the best views in resort. To avoid the crowds up here, go at lunchtime.	Grande Motte cable car
Stade de Lognan **	Wide, steep and usually well-groomed for the racing.	Merles
Myosotis *	Rolling run that with occasional steeper and narrower sections.	Aiguille Rouge
Pavots **	Scenic run with narrow path and piste sections. Can be icy or slushy in early/late season.	Chardons
Rocs **	Underneath Tommeuses section – normally a mogul run.	Tommeuses
Variente Rocs ***	A little steeper and more hardcore than the above run – a must for mogul fans!	Tommeuses

Tignes black pistes

Piste	Comments	Connections
Leisse *	A good first timer's black run – broad but not too steep, although it can get bumpy on the last 100 metres.	Leisse
Sache ***	The most difficult black in Tignes with a very steep and bumpy last section. It can get very rocky especially when there's not much snow so pick a route through and head for a reward of a beer in Les Brévières.	Marais and then **Cornice**
Silene ***	A mogul run that will take you to the Marais lift. Tackle this bump run in small sections, building up the number of moguls you manage each time.	Marais and then **Cornice**
Trolles **	A rolling fun run before it gets narrow, icy and bumpy all at once! Get into a rhythm and keep it going down this bit and the next steep before turning straight and schussing all the way into Le Lac.	Aeroski or Tufs, runs off **Crocus**

Val d'Isère red pistes

Piste	Comments	Connections
Arcelle ***	Steep entrance to a long run which can be a bit bullet proof early in the morning.	Manchet Express
Cascade **	Rolling run but with a mogul section at the side. Quiet enough to practise in peace.	Cascade Express
Cognon *	Short red with a flat section at the end.	Mangard
Fontaine Froide **	Nice run with varying pitches although loses its snow easily towards the end of the season.	Fontaine Froide
Fourche *	Just one short steep section otherwise a good alternative to the blues up here.	Datcha
Germain Mattis ***	Great winding road run which then drops down to join Piste 'L' down to the new Laisinant Express.	Laisinant Express then Aiglon or from Col de la Madeleine
Moraine *	Wide open and often quiet.	Cascade Express
Coupe de Monde - OK *	This is the location of the first of the season's World Cup Downhills in Europe. There are some steep sections on this run which are generally quite short.	Funival or Olympique

Piste	Comments	Connections
Orange **	Long and rolling run with the occasional steep or narrow drop, can get icy in the lower half.	Funival or Olympique
Piste 'M' **	A busy red running down from Solaise back to Val d'Isère. Although not difficult, the traffic and chopped up pistes can make it a tricky descent at times.	Plan
Plan **	Wider than above and generally kept in good condition.	Solaise, Solaise Express
Roches Combes des Géant *	Generally easy with one long steeper section although there are some uphill sections.	Montets
Semanmille **	Short rolling run that is often quiet.	Semanmille
Stade de Slalom	Pay €2 and check your speed on the timed slalom course.	Mont Blanc, Slalom
Signal ***	Only accessed by the Signal drag which can be a bit hairy in itself especially for boarders.	Signal
Triffolet ***	Gentle red that runs alongside the competition run. Lack of snow can make it bumpy.	Verte

Val d'Isère black pistes

Piste	Comments	Connections
3000 ***	Rarely open and usually bumpy when it is. Short but steep all the way down.	3000
Epaule du Charvet ***	Classic black when the conditions are good but normally full of moguls and ice. There's a long flat schuss at the end into Le Chatelard.	**Club des Sports** or **Grand Pré**
Face ***	Famous Olympic run down into the village. Winding and simple at the top, turning steeper for the bottom two thirds. Ski it straight after snowfall and you'll be in heaven.	Funival or Olympique
Forêt **	Narrow, steep, tree-lined and bumpy.	Fornet
Piste 'A' **	Narrow and often icy, although a quieter alternative to **Piste 'M'**.	**Plan**
Piste 'G' **	Access from skier's right of Folie Douce (> 87). Often closed for race training but if you can get on, you'll find a great run.	Daille
Raye **	Recently re-classified a black, it follows on from **Piste 'G'** above.	**Piste 'G'**
Tunnel***	Very rarely, if ever, open.	3000

Day trips

This section contains two of our favourites skiing itineraries in the Espace Killy. For a week's worth of downloadable day trips to keep you busy, visit our website **maddogski.com** for the following:

Day 1 – The Tignes tour

Day 2 – Les Brévières

Day 3 – Val d'Isère

Day 4 – The Solaise sprint

Day 5 – Le Fornet

Our day trips start around 10am and finish around 4pm. Timings are based on the pace of a confident red run skier and assume average length lift queues. Allow additional time if you are skiing more slowly or during school holidays when some lifts can have longer queues. If you are leaving the Tignes ski area, it is better to be less ambitious than to miss the last connecting lift home, which can result in having to take a taxi back from Val d'Isère.

Left/right directions assume you are heading down the hill or getting off the lift. All routes start from Val Claret or Le Lac. If you're staying elsewhere, it's relatively easy to adjust the first and last part of each itinerary.

Our researchers have worked hard to make these itineraries as accurate as possible but we do recommend that you always carry a piste map with you as pistes and routes can change from season to season.

Lift types

Lifts are shown with the symbols for the lift type:

Téléski Drag lift

Télésiège Chairlift

Télécabine Gondola

Téléphérique Cable car

Funicular Train

Les Brévières – the tree run

The day starts in Val Claret but you can join the itinerary from Le Lac as well. Take the Palafour lift from Le Lac and then the Aiguille Percée and join the rest of the itinerary there. There are various routes to Les Brévières, depending on your ability, so it's an ideal day for mixed abilities as you all meet at the bottom for lunch before taking the Sache gondola back up to the main ski area.

Lift	Comments
Tichot	Head down the short run to Grattalu lift.
Grattalu	From the top, ski down keeping to the left until you join **Lac**. Halfway down, take a left towards the Grand Huit lift - beware the flat bit nearer to this lift.
Grand Huit	From the top, head down and round on the **Perce-Neige** until you reach the Aiguille Percée lift.
Aiguille Percée	Go straight on and ski down **Corniche** and then take one of the following: **(i)** For one of the most demanding black runs in resort, take the first left onto **Sache** all the way down to Les Brévières. Or for a less difficult black run, take the nest left onto **Silène** which will take you onto the **Chardons** and then **Pavot** down to the village. **(ii)** For a mid-range challenge, then continue on **Corniche** until you get to the top of the Aiguille Rouge lift. Here, turn left onto **Myosotis**. This will eventually join up with **Chardons** and **Pavot**. **(iii)** Ski to the top of the Chaudannes lift and bear left onto **Rhododendron**. This will branch into **Mélèzes** which takes you down onto **Myrtilles**, a road run winding its way gently down to the village.

Lift	Comments
Lunch	Meet everyone and sit down for some much-needed refreshments at the l'Armailly (> 71) a 100m stroll across the bridge.
Sache ⬆	From the top of the Sache, head down the short stretch to Marais. This is one of the longest and slowest lifts in resort so if late, take the Aiguille Rouge for a quick return to the Tignes valley.
Marais ⬆	Ski down Cyclamen until you get to a cross-roads of pistes just after this take a right towards Merles, beware it is very flat and only by maintaining a fast speed will walking be avoided.
Merles ⬆	Take Merles lift up and at the top, make your way across the flat to the Grattalu and ski this down until you reach the Carline. Or alternatively, if it is not being used, down the Stade de Lognan-competition - a giant slalom course which has a great wide finish. Back down at the bottom, head over to the free Bollin lift.
Bollin ⬆	From here, head past the restaurant and down as far right as you can go, arriving in Val Claret centre for après-ski (> 76).

Le Fornet - into the back and beyond

The Fornet sector with its own glacier is for some reason, seldom skied by the masses and is known as the forgotten valley. Full of nice cruisy blues and reds with some spectacular views of the Isèran valley, this is the place to head to get away from it all.

Lift	Comments
Aeroski 🚠 **or Tufs** 🎿	From the top of Tovière, head down bearing left onto **Creux** until you reach the Mont Blanc chairlift on your right.
Mont Blanc 🎿	This lift takes you over the snowpark (➤ 30), if you want to pop in, double back on yourself, skiing out the bottom onto **Edelweiss** which will take you back to Mont Blanc. If the park isn't your thing, head left from the top down the short slope to the Marmottes lift. Stop before the lift for a coffee at Les Marmottes restaurant (➤ 88).
Marmottes 🎿	Head down to the bottom of the Grande Pré lift, take a left here and head down past Fontaine Froid lift and keep going down **Santons**. At the bottom, keep your speed up to clear the long flat stretch into Le Chatelard. Walk or push down until you reach the Solaise cable car on your left.

Lift	Comments
Solaise	From the top, take the rope drag and then ski under Datcha to the Glacier Express.
Glacier Express	Left off the chairlift to **Leissières**. Halfway down, stop at the Leissières Express – known as the 'up and over' with spectacular views and a stomach lurching summit.
Leissières Express	Right off the chair, turning back on yourself onto **Pont Abatte** staying as far left as you can. Ski all the way down, joining **Pré-Chemin** down to the bottom of Vallon de l'Isèran.
Lunch	Stop at the newly revamped **Le Signal (> 91)** for a slap up lunch.
Vallon de l'Isèran	At the top take Cascade Express.
Cascade Express	Ski down to the bottom of the T-bar on your right.

Lift	Comments
Montets	This is the highest point in the Fornet. From here, take **Roches** all the way down until you join **Combe du Géant** down to the bottom of Cema chair.
Cema	From the top, stay left and ski down onto any of the blue runs in front of you. You can take any route down with a choice of blues until you reach the Signal restaurant and lift station again. Ski to the right onto **Mangard** and cruise all the way back down to the village of Le Fornet.
Finish	To get back to Tignes, you have two options:
	(i) Take the Signal cable car then Vallon de l'Isèran back up and ski back to the up and over chair to Solaise. Then ski down to Val d'Isère village and take the Bellevarde Express up and then ski all the way to the Tommeuses lift and then down to Tignes
	(ii) Tired legs might want to catch the ski bus from Le Fornet to the centre of Val and then hop on the bus to La Daille. Here, get the Daille gondola up, ski the short distance to the Tommeuses and then either get the Aeroski down to Le Lac or ski the last part.

Where to find the best **food and drink,** from pizza to regional specialities to luxurious restaurants.

What you'll find in this chapter

One of the most enjoyable aspects of time off the slopes in Tignes, is time spent sampling the local Savoyard cuisine: a satisfying mix of cheese and meat to sate your appetite after a long day on the hill.

And when you can't possibly eat any more cheese, there are plenty of restaurants specialising in other types of food from Belgian to Vietnamese to good old English pub grub. Carnivores can look forward to fantastic steaks at reasonable prices in most restaurants. Remember that the French prefer their steak (and lamb and duck) less well cooked so if you normally have your steak rare, order it medium (> 58).

Many places offer Savoyard specialities (> 60) which are perfect for a group meal – especially if a selection of dishes are ordered.

Drinking is not cheap in any French ski resort and prices in Tignes are on par with London. Drinking beer and wine is cheaper than downing spirits which come at a premium up here. Food prices may vary but drink prices are pretty consistent unless you find yourself in an upmarket hotel bar.

What's at steak?

Blue	bleu
Rare	saignant (pronounced 'sanyon')
Medium	à point
Well-done	bien cuit
Steak tartare	raw minced beef mixed with onions, herbs and spices
Pavé	thick cut rump steak
Entrecôte	similar to rib eye – fatty but flavoursome
Faux-filet	similar to sirloin
Filet	similar to fillet steak
Côte de boeuf	a huge side of beef normally served on the bone with sauces and shared between two or more people

Show some respect

Hundreds of glaciers have melted in the last 150 years.

Join our Respect the Mountain campaign to save those still standing.

Buy a green wristband and visit **respectthemountain.com** to discover how you can make a difference.

respectthemountain.com

Savoyard food

Beaufort	a hard cheese made from the milk of the local mahogany-coloured Beaufort cows.
Chevrotin	a soft, almost sweet goats cheese that is perfect after a meal with some wine or port.
Crozets	tiny squares of pasta that are traditionally served in a sauce of local cheese, ham and cream.
Diots	local sausages – usually quite a strong flavour – in plain, cheese or cabbage variations – definitely an acquired taste.
Fondue	either a bubbling cauldron of oil that you cook chunks of meat in or else a mix of cheeses and spirits to dip bread into. Normally ordered for two or more.
Raclette	a grill with a large lump of cheese is brought to your table. As the cheese melts, scrape it onto cold meats, potatoes and salad. Normally ordered for two or more.
Reblochon	a local cheese that has a delicious flavour and an easily recognisable pungent smell – you'll smell it in all Savoyard restaurants. Originally made with the milk from the second milking (the rebloche).
Pierre chaude	a hot stone on which you cook a variety of meats on your table. Sprinkle the stone with salt before cooking to prevent sticking.
Tartiflette	an extremely satisfying mix of potato, bacon, cream and reblochon cheese which is then baked in the oven. A variation; Tartichèvre is made with goat's cheese. Normally ordered for two or more.
Tomme de Savoie	an ivory-coloured, delicate cheese often made with skimmed milk and therefore lower in fat.

Savoyard drinks

Chartreuse	drink it as a spirit or also nice when added to hot chocolate (green chaud).
Demi	beer is generally drunk in halves in France – sometimes served with peach syrup (demi pêche) – much nicer than it sounds!
Eau de vie	a digestif that is supposed to help digestion… if you like drinking something akin to petrol…
Génépi	famous for its local digestive values (when taken in moderation!), this local digestif is made from the local flower Génépi. Picking is strictly controlled and when you're offered a homemade bottle of the stuff, it is so nice you can see why!
Kir	an aperitif glass of white wine with a fruit liqueur added – usually cassis (blackcurrant), mure (blackberry) or framboise (raspberry).
Pression	draft lager.
Mutzig	super strong beer.
Vin chaud	hot, mulled wine.

Food and drink

Vegetarian options

Being vegetarian in the Savoie can be difficult – pizza, pasta, salad and fondues (all cheese based) will be the mainstay of the gourmet experience. It becomes a lot more flexible if you eat fish but many Tignes restaurants just don't get vegetarianism.

Savoyard cuisine excels in cheese and there are some great dishes such as salade de chevre chaud (goats cheese salad) and cheese fondues and raclettes to be sampled – all made out of local cheeses.

We've tried and tested the vegetarian dishes in all of the restaurants reviewed in this section and if we think they've made an effort with their dishes on offer, we've given them a **V** to save you having bad meals.

Children

Children are welcome in all restaurants and most places will have a special kids' menu or half portions on offer. We've included a selection of particularly good family-friendly restaurants in the **Children** chapter (**>** 103).

Budget meals and take-aways

Menu prices vary massively but you can usually tell by the appearance of a restaurant whether it will break the bank or not. Hotel restaurants tend to be pricier than the independents but even with these, a fixed price menu can be good value.

If you're looking for something cheap, look out for pizza restaurants or the English bars often offer budget

meals. If you want water with your meal, tap water here is perfectly safe to drink (and as it's from the mountains, tastes good too) – ask for a carafe d'eau for free water.

For take-aways, see **>** 72.

Resort restaurants

There are restaurants for all budgets in the different villages of Tignes but the biggest choice is in Val Claret and Le Lac. Whilst it's advisable to book ahead for the more popular restaurants, it is generally easy to walk in and get a table. The exceptions to this are busy times such as Christmas, New Year and school holidays (French and English half-terms take up most of February).

Our absolute favourites...and why

These are resort restaurants that our researchers return to time and time again.

L'Armailly > 71	The huge and varied menu makes this a perfect lunch stop or even dinner for every night of the week.
Bagus Café > 68	Savoyard restaurant with a north African twist serving pizzas, pastas and tagines.
Brasero > 70	Homemade pies, breakfast rolls and their butcher's block are more than enough reason to eat here.
Le Caveau > 66	Cosy underground restaurant serving a fusion of French and Asian cuisine.
Clin d'Oeil > 69	Intimate restaurant serving an inspired menu that changes regularly.
Couloir > 67	Steak house upstairs in this popular bar – try the 500g Yeti steak.
Escale Blanche > 70	Large popular place that's good for families. The salads here are fantastic.
L'Etoile des Neiges > 71	Oysters and scallops as well as pizzas, paninis and pastas.
Saint Jacques > 68	Belgian restaurant worth visiting for its beer list and seafood.
Tignes Cuisine > 73	Take-away/delivery meals including curries and Asian dishes. Or try a pasty during après-ski.

Tignes – Le Lac

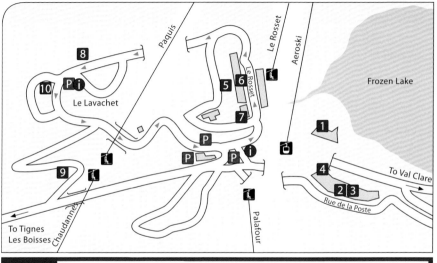

Key:

ℹ Maison de Tignes
P Parking

1. Le Lagon Leisure Centre

2. Bagus Café
3. Café Rouge
4. Calèche

5. Le Chalet
6. Clin d'Oeil
7. Escale Blanche

8. Le Brasero
9. La Ferme des 3 Capucines
10. TC's Bar/Lavachet Lounge

Tignes – Val Claret

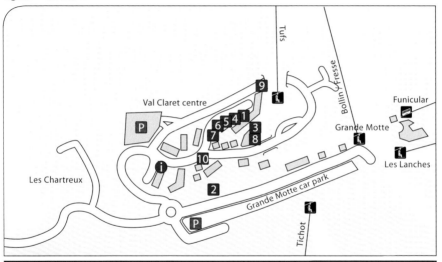

Key:

- ℹ Le Nevada
- Ⓟ Parking
- 1. Le Caveau
- 2. Chalet Bouvier
- 3. Le Coffee
- 4. Couloir
- 5. La Pignatta
- 6. Saint Jacques
- 7. Crowded House
- 8. Drop Zone
- 9. Fish Tank
- 10. Melting Pot

Food and drink Resort restaurants

65

How to read our reviews

Resort restaurants (> 66) and bars (> 74) are listed in alphabetical order by village. Mountain restaurants are alphabetical by resort.

Val Claret
Le Caveau
T +33 (0)4 79 06 52 32

Centre, 7.30pm – late, band starts at 11pm.
Cosy underground restaurant behind a small wooden door, this restaurant is hugely popular with visitors and locals. The cuisine is a mix between local dishes and Asian fusion creating dishes such as quail fillet with grape sauce and sesame (€28) and salmon and

How to read our reviews:

 Budget: most main course prices are under €10

 Mid-range: main course prices range from €11-20

 Expensive: most main courses are mainly over €20

 Good vegetarian choice

 Our absolute Mad Dog favourites

tuna brochettes with garlic and wasabi (€25). Set menus range between €27 and €33 (vegetarian menu - €23) for three courses. There are two sittings (7.30pm and 9.30pm) – book the later one to be entertained by the house band from 11pm.

Chalet Bouvier
T +33 (0)4 79 06 99 90

Grande Motte road, inside the Ecrin du Val Claret hotel, 7-11pm.
Upmarket Savoyard restaurant headed by top chef Jean-Michel Bouvier. The food is high-quality

versions of traditional Savoie dishes (from €14 per person) and more inventive flavours of dark, rich meaty dishes. Our favourites include the starter of foie gras (€32 for two people) or beef tartare (€22). Attracting a slightly older clientele, this restaurant would be ideal for a quieter, more romantic night out.

Le Coffee – Evolution 2
T +33 (0)4 79 40 06 05

Centre, piste-side opposite tunnel, 8.30am-7pm.
At the bottom of the Val Claret piste, this café is perfectly placed as a pit-stop for lunch – serving burgers, paninis, salads, pasta and main dishes. Sit in a comfy deckchair in the sun or inside

during bad weather. The café also does a good breakfast which is served until 11am.

Couloir
T +33 (0)4 79 06 32 64

Centre (upstairs in the Couloir bar), 7-10.30pm.
This bar-come-steak house is one of the most popular haunts in the resort. The bar (> 76) is usually jumping, whilst upstairs you can eat your fill. Mainly centred around meat dishes such as the 500g Yeti steak (€25), kangaroo fillet (€17) or the high-altitude beef which is cooked at the table in a frying pan (€16), this place is a meat-eater's paradise. Tapas and vegetarian choices also available.

La Pignatta
T +33 (0)4 79 06 32 97

Centre, next to Saint Jacques, 12-3pm, 6-11pm.
Family-run Italian restaurant with an excellent range of food including pizza, pasta and Savoyard specialities. For carnivores, the steaks are first-rate with a large choice of cuts as well as accompaniments (entrecôte grille with a choice of sauces, €18). Vegetarians are catered for too with a large pizza menu and some interesting salads. It's a comfortable place with a rustic, cosy atmosphere. There are several long tables so it's ideal for large groups.

Le Lac

Saint Jacques

T +33 (0)4 79 06 48 33

Centre, next to Precision, 12-2.30pm, 7-11pm.

This Belgian restaurant is another firm favourite with its range of seafood, fish dishes and speciality beers. Staples of moules mariniere washed down with glasses of Kwak beer are our favourites but we also like the tuna sashimi with avocado starter (€18), the main meals of king prawns in garlic (€23) and fillet steak topped with fois gras (€34). Three course menus from €25 and the wine from around €19 a bottle. Known as a restaurant that'll kick-start a long boozy night and popular with a younger crowd.

Bagus Café

T +33 (0)4 79 06 49 75

Rue de la Poste, halfway up hill, 12-3pm 7-10pm.

A sister restaurant of the Pignatta in Val Claret (➤ 67), the Bagus marks itself out by introducing a north African twist to its otherwise Savoyard menu. That means that alongside the tasty wood-fired pizzas, pasta and meat dishes, you can find a selection of tagines (lamb/chicken for €18.50 or king prawns for €22). Vegetarian dishes consist of a range of pastas and pizzas as well as vegetarian lasagne for €12. A vibrant restaurant ideal for younger groups.

Café Rouge

T +33 (0)4 79 40 09 23

Rue de la Poste, halfway up the hill, 7-9.30pm.

A new restaurant last season, Café Rouge serves up a meaty Savoyard menu including meat skewers (beef and duck from €15) that you cook yourself, king prawns in Armagnac (€17) and fondues from €14. The highlight of the starters is the pricey but luscious snails in blue cheese sauce in the salade du chef (€12).

Calèche

T +33 (0)4 79 06 50 80

Inside the Palafour arcade, 10am-2.30pm, 7-10pm.

A Savoyard restaurant that is open for breakfast and serves a little later into the night than many. The entrance to the restaurant is inside the shopping arcade but it also has an outside terrace facing the frozen lake. As well as their menu of three courses for €17.50, their à la carte menu has some pleasant dishes including salmon lasagne (€14), grilled king prawns (€22.50) and entrecôte steak (€18).

Le Chalet

T +33 (0)4 79 06 34 36
W campanules.com

In the Campanules hotel, Le Lac Rosset, up past the Aiguille Percee hotel and round the top corner, 12-2.30pm, 6-11pm.

An elegant first-class restaurant in the traditional wooden setting of a large hotel situated behind Le Rosset. The cuisine is divine with dishes such as roast lamb cooked until so tender, it almost falls apart, grilled lobster and Charolais beef. The food is well-presented and the menu changes often. The only downside is that the drinks and wine are rather expensive compared to the food. Reservations advised.

Clin d'Oeil

T +33 (0)4 79 06 59 10

Le Rosset, halfway along the shopping terrace, 7-10.30pm (lunchtimes by reservation).

A bit of a hidden gem, this intimate restaurant offers an elaborate take on French cuisine and a frequently changing menu of local produce. Dishes have included fricassee of snails with baby leeks, stewed garlic and dried beef (€12), leg of guinea fowl stuffed with scampi (€21) followed by fried chocolate snowball with caramel and pear mousse. Food like this is difficult to find elsewhere in resort. Booking is advisable as the cosy restaurant only seats about 30 people.

Escale Blanche

T +33 (0)4 79 06 45 50

Centre, next to Maison de Tignes, 6.30am-10.30pm.

A varied menu, from regional specialities to international dishes to generous salads. The restaurant is reasonably priced and comfortable with very friendly service. Suitable for all the family as food is served non-stop throughout the day (and until 11pm). With a very big south-facing terrace just across from the piste, it's particularly good for lunch. We'd recommend the Escale Blanche salad (€6.90/11) – a satisfying combination of ham, egg, goats cheese, bacon and walnuts.

Lavachet

Le Brasero

T +33 (0)4 79 06 30 60

W brasero.co.uk

Centre, to left of bus stop, 12-2.30pm, 7-11pm.

Opened in the 2005/6 season, this bar/restaurant has a large and varied menu and is perfect for lunch or dinner. Highlights for lunch include their homemade pies such as tandoori chicken (€12), hot sandwiches (€7) or salads (from €10). Dinner is a mix of local and international cuisine with dishes like crozets de Savoie (€13), salad du mer (€11/15) or their famous butcher's block mixed grill (€18).

La Ferme des 3 Capucines

T +33 (0)4 79 06 35 10

On the road out of Tignes from Lavachet, just before you meet the main mountain road, 12-2pm, 7-10pm.

'La Ferme' (the farm); this restaurant lives up to its name and is the highest winter farm for miles. Whilst the smell of farmyards might not be for everyone, the unique atmosphere makes for a memorable evening out. And what better place to eat food straight from the farmyard out back? The set menu here normally involves several courses of traditional fare and gives you a lot for your money.

TC's Bar/Lavachet Lounge

T +33 (0)4 79 06 46 46
W tcsbar.com

Centre, to the left of Snowfun,
3-10pm (from 10am at weekends).
The bar snacks at these English-
run bars (> 80) extends to
homemade burgers (€10), all day
breakfasts and a dish of the day.

Les Boisses
Le Marais

T +33 (0)4 79 06 40 06
W hotel-le-marais.com

Top road of Les Boisses,
12-2.30pm, 7-10pm.
The restaurant and conservatory
of this hotel is an elegant place to
eat, or sit on the sunny terrace for

lunch and have amazing views of
Lac du Chevril. The menu consists
of dishes such as cake of pig
trotters, frog legs and crispy fillet
of sea perch. The restaurant is
a little difficult to get to from the
upper villages but it's worth a visit
if you're in the area.

Les Brévières
L'Armailly

T +33 (0)4 79 06 41 82

Main road, opposite the piste,
12-2.30pm, 7-10pm.
A shady terrace with a large
restaurant/bar area inside makes
it an ideal location to take in the
charm of the snow covered fir
trees in Les Brévières. The huge
menu includes dishes such

as brochettes of king prawns
and scallops (€23), a variety of
pizzas (from €11) and assiette de
l'Armailly (€16). The décor inside
is typically Alpine and there are
lots of long tables with benches
which easily accommodate
groups.

L'Etoiles des Neiges

T +33 (0)4 79 06 41 16

On piste, opposite Sache chairlift,
8.30am-6.30pm.
Located at the bottom of the piste
into Les Brévières, opposite the
Sache gondola, you can't miss this
large restaurant. Oysters (six for
€15, 12 for €28) and scallops are
a speciality as well as pizzas (from
€13.50), pasta (€15) and meat

dishes and crêpes for dessert. Inside there is a big fire place and outside a very big south-facing terrace. There is a snack hut selling paninis, chips then waffles. Some people will be surprised by the prices in comparison to the other restaurants although if you stick to the normal fare, you can eat reasonably cheaply.

Take-aways

Most supermarkets (> 109) sell take-away food and spit-roasted chickens. Many also rent raclette and fondue equipment.

Daffy's Café
T +33 (0)4 79 06 38 75
W tex-mex.fr

Val Claret centre, Le Grand Tichot.
This Mexican restaurant offers a take-away menu of quesadillas (from €6.75), nachos (€9) and salads (€9). There is also a children's menu for €5.40 of burgers or chicken nuggets.

Pizza Mick
T +33 (0)4 79 06 30 97

Lavachet centre.
Wood-fired pizzas, rotisserie

chicken, chips and sweet crêpes are served by this popular pizza take-away. There is a small amount of seating inside.

Royal Kebab
T +33 (0)6 19 27 45 15

Val Claret centre, up the steps to the left of Sherpa.
Kebabs and burgers – the only place you can get food at 2am.

SOS Pizza
T +33 (0)4 79 06 08 08

Le Lac, Rue de la Poste, opposite the Post Office.
Choice of small or large pizzas with a variety of toppings from €6.60. Delivery anywhere in resort costs 80c per pizza. Beer and wine is also sold.

Tignes Cuisine
T: +33 (0)4 79 06 44 44

Le Lac Rosset, end of shopping terrace.

The best take-away/delivery in resort will deliver to your door a range of dishes from spicy curries (from €11) to Chinese duck and pancakes (€14) to BBQ ribs (€14.50). Vegetarian options include vegetable versions of all the curries or ask the chef what's on offer that day. Wine and beer is also sold. If you pop by the shop at après-ski, you can often grab a freshly homemade pasty to go with your beer.

Most of the restaurants serving pizzas also offer take-aways:

Petit Savoyard, Val Claret centre
T +33 (0)4 79 06 36 23

La Pignatta, Val Claret centre
T +33 (0)4 79 06 32 97 (➤ 67)

Pizza 2000, Val Claret centre
T +33 (0)4 79 06 38 49

Le Bagus, Rue de la Poste, Le Lac
T +33 (0)4 79 06 49 75 (➤ 68)

Arbina, Le Rosset, Le Lac
T +33 (0)4 79 06 39 02

Escale Blanche, Le Rosset, Le Lac
T +33 (0)4 79 06 45 50 (➤ 70)

of friends; an all-night free bus makes this easy.

Many places kick off for après-ski around 4pm and close around 1am with the nightclubs staying open until 4am.

Après-ski & nightlife

Although Tignes is generally considered to have a far quieter nightlife that neighbouring Val d'Isère, things are improving all the time. And what the resort lacks in heaving raucous bars everywhere you look, it makes up for with cheaper drinks prices and places to sit. Brit pubs to cosy French wine bars to pumping Swedish frenzies mean there is generally something to suit most tastes. Bar crawls are an essential part of your stay in Tignes, if not as part of the Monday night ritual, then on your own or with a group

Our absolute favourites... and why

Alpaka > 78	A cosy hotel bar with comfy sofas and fantastic cocktails.
Crowded House > 76	Cool, snowboarder hangout with big parties and lively atmosphere.
Couloir > 76	40 flavoured vodkas, live music and DJs make this bar the place to go for a fun night out.
Drop Zone > 77	French bar where you can play pool or dance to a live band.
Fish Tank > 77	Situated at the bottom of the piste, this terrace is great place to unwind after a day's skiing.
Jam Bar > 79	The popular Jam Bar spreads its wings and takes its formula onwards and upwards to new premises this winter.
Lavachet Lounge > 79	Non-smoking laid-back lounge bar with free internet, TV, cocktails, smoothies and cakes.
Melting Pot > 78	Popular nightclub with a music policy that manages to steer clear of euro-pop.
TC's Bar > 80	Friendly and welcoming bar serving up beer, bar food and laughs.

Food and drink Après-ski

Live music

Val Claret

Couloir (> 76)

Drop Zone (> 77)

Fish Tank (> 77)

Le Lac

Alpaka (> 78)

Jam Bar (> 79)

Le Lavachet

Brasero (> 79)

Scotty's (> 80)

Val Claret

Le Blue Girl

T +33 (0)4 79 06 51 53

Centre, Sefcotel building, from 11pm.

French euro-pop techno with a sprinkling of Rn'B songs that will get you on the dance floor. Blue Girl is also famous for its popular weekly sexy show – female strippers (which, it has to be said, may not be for everyone).

Crowded House

T +33 (0)4 79 06 34 34

Centre, underneath Hotel Curling, from 4pm.

This is much more than your average hotel bar and the Crowded House certainly lives up to its name and attracts a young mass of mainly British season workers and pro snowboarders. Well known for wacky fancy dress evenings – be prepared for a big night out.

Couloir

T +33 (0)4 79 06 32 64

Centre, from 4pm.

The Couloir is the place to go for a great night of dancing to one of their many DJs or bands. Usually jumping, it is perfect as a pre-club venue where you can get in the mood by sampling one of the 40 exotically flavoured vodkas, some of the best whiskeys in resort or one of their delicious cocktails.

Also popular for après-ski when you can pop in for some tapas or paninis with your beer. Wi-Fi available.

Drop Zone
T +33 (0)4 79 06 32 59

Centre, Sefcotel building, from 4pm.

This French-owned bar is a popular place to play pool and listen to the French bands that frequently play. Happy hour is from 4-7pm and food is also served. Wi-Fi available.

Fish Tank
T +33 (0)4 79 06 46 60

Centre, near Tufs chairlift, from 8.30am.

The British-owned Fish Tank is located in the centre of Val Claret on the edge of the main **Claret** piste into the area. It is a popular place to relax après-ski, either on the large south-facing terrace or inside. After dinner the bar is buzzing with both season workers and holiday makers and is the place to head to watch sport, play pool or listen to live music (on offer twice a week). Food served all day.

Grizzly's Bar
T +33 (0)4 79 06 34 17

Centre, from 4pm.

Grizzly's is the best place in Tignes to experience a traditional Alpine ambience, albeit an expensive one. It's popular during après-ski to sit on the handcrafted wooden benches on the terrace around the open fire; if it gets cold you can snuggle up under a fur throw or move inside the very cosy and ornately decorated bar and warm up by the fire. Charcuterie and cheese platters available from €12 to accompany your drinks.

Melting Pot
T +33 (0)4 79 06 35 21

Centre, from 10pm.

Popular nightclub with the Brits due to the many guest DJ nights, if you've baulked at the cheesiness of the other clubs then this is the place for you. With an up-to-date music policy of funk and drum'n'bass it attracts a lot of season workers and holiday makers alike. Ladies' night with free champagne on Saturday evenings is a great way to start (or end) the week.

Le Studio
T +33 (0)4 79 08 57 44

Centre, Sefcotel building, from 4pm.

A comfortable French bar where you can mix with the locals, watch sport (mainly French) and enjoy a Pastis or two.

Le Lac
Alpaka
T +33 (0)4 79 06 45 30
W alpaka.com

Montee du Rosset, up the road beside Le Refuge hotel, from 4pm.
This hotel bar has a cosy relaxed feel with lots of comfy sofas, just like being in your own living room.

Cocktails are a speciality and the range is enormous. Champagne nights and shots nights (free one with every drink bought) are a weekly occurrence and both attract the crowds. Sport is also shown on the big screen at the weekends. Wi-Fi available.

Embuscade
T +33 (0)4 79 06 59 51

Rue de la Poste, from 4pm.
This out of the way bar at the top of Rue de la Poste is a nice hideaway to go and chat to the French locals, play pool or check your emails. A pleasant place to hang out with great views over the lake. Wi-Fi available.

Jacks Le Bowling
T +33 (0)4 79 06 54 84

Bec Rouge, from 10pm.
Situated within the bowling alley, Jacks specialises in 80's and dance music – both English and French. If you don't take your music too seriously, it's perfect for a dance and a whirl around the pole.

Jam Bar
T +33 (0)4 79 06 30 61
W jambar.net

Le Lac, open from breakfast.
The Jam Bar has enjoyed an extremely popular couple of years and looks set to only improve on their friendly bustling atmosphere with fantastic breakfasts and bar food throughout the day. There are rumours they will be seeking bigger premises for this season – well worth checking out!

Lavachet
Brasero
T +33 (0)4 79 06 30 60
W brasero.co.uk

Next to the bus stop, from 10am.
A popular bar with live bands playing regularly, sport shown on the flat screen TV and drinks promo nights. Free Wi-Fi for customers, sofas and a terrace for lazing on in warm weather makes this a relaxed bar to spend time in. Food is served in their bar and restaurant (> 77).

Lavachet Lounge
T +33 (0)4 79 08 46 13

Up steps in front of Snow Fun, from 11am (4pm at the weekends).
The only non-smoking bar in the resort, this laid-back lounge bar is the place to come to chill, check your emails and watch TV from the comfortable leather sofas. Their drinks list includes smoothies, milkshakes, cocktails and a good selection of wines. Board games, cards and a book swap library means this place has more a relaxing café feel to it but this is a refreshing change in Tignes. Free Wi-Fi and two computers for customers customers to use.

Scotty's

T +33 (0)4 79 06 63 20

Opposite bus stop, from 4pm (9am at weekends).

A large pub-style bar attached to the Mark Warner Tovière hotel. The bar often has live music, theme nights and a generous happy hour. It's quite dark inside but this just adds to the atmosphere, which is very similar to a pub back in Blighty. They also serve food and there are often good value deals to be had. Free Wi-Fi to customers.

TC's Bar

T +33 (0)4 79 05 46 46

W tcsbar.com

Up the steps in front of Snow Fun, from 3pm (from 10am at weekends).

The 'local' for many of the resort's French and British workers, this small and friendly bar has an English pub feel and is a welcoming place. Try the special Mutzig beer that they serve – a strong brew renowned in resort for messy nights. Sky TV, Wi-Fi and a computer is on offer for customers and bar food is also served (> 71).

Les Brévières

Underground Bar

T +33 (0)4 79 06 53 39

W chaletchardons.com

Underneath Chalet Chardons, from 6pm.

This bar is attached to the budget hotel Chalet Chardons. As well as a discount card for guests, the bar also runs theme nights every night of the week including a karaoke, quiz and table football nights.

Mountain restaurants

This section reviews every mountain restaurant shown on the Espace Killy piste map whether good, bad or indifferent, although you'll find more information on our favourite places (full reviews on **maddogski.com**). The numbers next to each restaurant review correspond to the numbers on the mountain restaurant map (> 82).

In each review, we give you a price guide to the restaurant as well as their contact details and which lifts to take to get to them. If non-skiers can access them from Tignes, we tell you that too. Almost every restaurant opens and closes around the same time as the lifts and serves lunch from 12-3pm (longer in self-service places) although a few will open for groups in the evening. We'd recommend booking ahead for some of the more upmarket restaurants as they fill up quickly at lunchtimes.

The worst that can be said about some restaurants is that they seem complacent, with unimaginative menus and unremarkable food. Others make a real effort and even old favourites such as spag bol, carbonara and pizza are tasty and filling. However they almost all have stunning views, so even if we don't recommend them for food, they can be good for a drink. And if you want to save your precious cash for something else, on > 99 we tell you where you can pick up picnic supplies that will keep you going all day. We list the restaurants

alphabetically by resort below:

Tignes > 85
Val d'Isère > 86

For the key to the symbols we use, see > 66.

Val d'Isère

1 Les Crozets
2 Edelweiss
3 Le Signal
4 La Datcha
5 Cabinet de Neige
6 Les Clochetons
7 Le Bar de l'Ouillette
8 La Taniere
9 Le Bellevarde
10 Les Marmottes
11 La Folie Douce/
La Fruitière
12 Tête de Solaise/
Le Trifollet
13 Les Tuffs

Val d'Isère
valdisere.com

Tignes

1 La Tovière
2 Le Chalet du Bollin
3 Panoramic
4 Le Palet
5 La Savouna
6 Alpage/Lo Soli

Our absolute favourites... and why

L'Arolay > 90	Not really a mountain restaurant but one that makes a great mountain lunch when in Le Fornet.
Alpage/Lo Soli > 85	Sample some of the rustic yet tantalising cuisine at the table-service restaurant here (Lo Soli).
Edelweiss > 90	Romantic restaurant hidden in the trees in Le Fornet with roaring log fire inside and a terrace with stunning views outside.
Folie Douce > 87	Self-service with large terrace that is usually filled with dancing skiers.
La Fruitière > 87	Gastronomic restaurant linked to the Folie Douce serving unusual gourmet dishes.
Les Marmottes > 88	Perhaps one of the best value self-service mountain restaurants with a sun-trap of a terrace.
Le Signal > 91	Popular restaurant that has been recently renovated into a modern and chic lunch stop.
La Tovière > 86	Self-service that offers basic fare but in large portions. Also a good place to meet friends.
Panoramic > 85	Two restaurants, waffle stall and a terrace with views over the glacier.

Tignes

Alpage/Lo Soli 6
T +33 (0)4 79 06 07 42

Lifts/Pedestrian: Chaudannes.
The Alpage is a self-service restaurant serving basic dishes such as omelettes (€10), pasta (€9) and steak (€16). Lo Soli, however is definitely worth a visit for a long lunch in the mountains. Serving up an innovative take on traditional cuisine such as their pot au feu of three meats (€20), house tartiflette (€27) and, for vegetarians, a millefeuille of vegetables (€12). The food is generally rustic but filling and satisfying, especially on a cold day.

Le Chalet du Bollin 2
T +33 (0)4 79 06 46 44

Lifts: Bollin or from Prariond or Piste 'H'.
Fairly basic lunch stop with an open fire inside, which is very welcome on colder days, or a terrace for warmer weather.

Le Palet 4
T +33 (0)4 79 06 46 06

Lifts: Tichot, Grattalu.
Usual self-service place with good spaghetti bolognaise (€10), tartiflette (€15) and lasagne (€13). A real suntrap, and an ideal place to sit and watch the world ski by.

Panoramic 3
T +33 (0)4 79 06 47 21

Lifts/Pedestrian: Funicular Grande Motte.
With clear views of the glacier, the Panoramic has a large self-service restaurant with an enormous sunny terrace that sells waffles in various hot sticky flavours. There is also a lovely little restaurant (mid-range to expensive) serving a limited but interesting menu (for example foie gras and scampi of langoustine). The chef cooks all the food in the centre of the restaurant next to the open fire. Evening booking available.

La Savouna 5

T +33 (0)4 79 06 33 80

Lifts: Palafour.

This is a pretty basic self-service restaurant providing the usual pastas and steaks. Portion sizes are healthy so it is a good enough place to stop for a carb or protein fill up.

La Tovière 1

T +33 (0)4 79 06 35 05

Lifts: Aeroski, Tufs, Pedestrian: Aeroski.

Located at the top of the Tovière, this restaurant has a separate drink and snack bar as well as a self-service restaurant. In good weather, they crank up the music and the waffle stall to draw the crowds onto their sunny terrace. Their self-service restaurant offers the usual ham and chips (€10), ribs (€10) and spaghetti (€6) in large portions to fill you up. Its location between Val and Tignes makes this a fitting place to stop for coffee (good double espresso) or a beer before taking your last run of the day. In the evenings, groups (minimum 15 people) can book the restaurant for an evening meal and be transported by snow cat.

Val d'Isère

Le Bellevarde 9

T +33 (0)4 79 06 05 76

Lifts: Olympique, Funival.

For a restaurant in such an amazing location the food and service can be a little dull although the portions are large and the prices reasonable – omelettes (€8.60), Spaghetti (€10) and hamburger (€9.50). If warm enough, sit on the terrace and admire the stunning view of the Charvet peak and the famous Pisteur's Couloir.

Les Clochetons 6

T +33 (0)4 79 41 13 11

Lifts: Olympique, Pistes: Epaule de Charvet, Santons, Pedestrian:

Train Bleu then walk over the road.
After Santons or the off-piste Tour
de Charvet, this is a welcome
place to stop for a rest, a drink or
a bite to eat. The food is not cheap
but the high quality means it is still
good value.

La Datcha 4
T +33 (0)4 79 06 21 14

*Lifts: Datcha, Madeleine Express,
Glacier Express.*
Not the cheapest place
considering it is a self-service
café but it's a good suntrap and
somewhere to enjoy a vin chaud
and watch the world go by.

La Folie Douce 11
T +33 (0)4 79 06 01 47

Lifts: Tufs, Aeroski, Fresse.
If you're looking for a party on
the mountain, this is the place
to come. A large terrace usually
packed with jiving skiers, some on
tables, whilst the bands play down
to them from the rooftops. Come
for the self-service food which is
standard but the party atmosphere
is a definite must-try experience.
Just remember to go back to
Tignes before the Tommeuses lift
shuts!

La Fruitière 11
T +33 (0)4 79 06 07 17

Lifts: Tufs, Aeroski, Fresse.
A gastronomic restaurant linked
to the Folie Douce serving a menu
of innovative dishes such as duck
shepherd's pie with raspberry
(€22), polenta with escalope of foie
gras (€23) and rabbit with morel
and spaghetti (€19). There is an
imaginative selection of cheeses (five
varieties with salad costs €17) and
you can eat on the terrace or inside.
Some people may go here to be
seen – but the food alone is worth
a detour. You are often given a free
génépi at the end of the meal.

Les Marmottes 10
T +33 (0)4 79 06 05 08

Lifts: Mont Blanc.

This is the best value self-service mountain restaurant in the Val ski area with generous portions and brisk service. Main meals are mostly under €10 and plat du jours include dishes such as rabbit in mustard sauce (€8.60). Sit on the sun-drenched terrace with a coffee (€2) or beer (from €3) and gaze at the splendid view of the Bellevarde.

Le Bar de l'Ouillette 7
T +33 (0)4 79 41 94 74

Lifts: Solaise or Solaise Express, Tête de Solaise or Terrasse.

Appetising sandwiches, delicious pastries and a wicked assortment of cakes are brought up fresh every day from the famous Maison Chevallot bakers in Val d'Isère.

The Sun Bar (not on the piste)
T +33 (0)4 79 41 16 61

Lifts: Next to Olympique.
Great location by the Olympique cable car and with a lovely sunny terrace. Food is pretty basic but they seem to do well enough serving standard dishes such as pasta and lasagne.

Le Tanière 8
T +33 (0)4 79 08 80 26

Lifts: Olympique, Bellevarde Express.

Its location halfway down the famous Olympic run, the **Face**, means that if you can negotiate the (normally icy) piste then you will be rewarded with a crowd-free restaurant and an excellent lunch.

Tête de Solaise/Cabinet de Neige 5
T +33 (0)4 79 06 03 04

Lifts: Solaise or Solaise Express, Lac.
The food and service at this hut has improved enormously recently and a new 360° bar on the huge terrace makes this a nice lunch stop when skiing the Solaise.

Le Trifollet 12
T +33 (0)4 79 41 96 99

Lifts: La Daille.
Renowned for its pizzas, Le Trifollet is an excellent place to stop for lunch although is can get very busy and the staff can seem rather overstretched.

Les Tuffs 13
T +33 (0)4 79 06 25 01

Lifts: Between bottom of Etroits and Funival.
This restaurant is on the piste but all the way down in La Daille serving snacks, lunch and dinner menu.

Val d'Isère – Le Fornet

L'Arolay 4

T +33 (0)4 79 06 11 68

*Lifts: in Le Fornet about 200m
down the road on the left.*
This isn't really a mountain
restaurant but it's worth the
short walk in ski boots. There are
sweeping views down the Isère
gorge and into the valley below.
Inside there is an open fire and
an authentic mountain chalet
feel. Prices are more reasonable
than some of the other mountain
restaurants (probably because of
the walk) so you can have a slap-
up lunch without worrying about
the bill.

Les Crozets 1

T +33 (0)4 79 41 17 90

Lifts: Fornet cable car.
Les Crozets is a good-value self-
service restaurant with a snack
bar menu selling pasta, omelettes
and steak.

Edelweiss 2

T +33 (0)6 10 28 70 64

Lifts: Fornet cable car.
The terrace looks out over the
trees and down the valley onto Val
d'Isère. Inside there is a beautiful
log fire with flames dancing away,
just waiting to warm you up. If
we could get poetic then the
Edelweiss would be the place
that inspires us, instead we are
content with the mouth-watering
food that is on the menu. Don't
go for what you know; try instead
one of the more unusual dishes
like the pig liver casserole lazily
followed by the best raspberry
and vanilla pudding you are ever
likely to taste. Is this our favourite
restaurant? On a sunny day, after
skiing powder …yes.

Le Signal 3

T: +33 (0)4 79 06 03 38
W: lesignalvaldisere.com

  Table service

Self service

Lifts: Fornet cable car.
Recently renovated, the Signal
now comprises of a modern and
chic restaurant, a self-service
bar as well as a take-away point
outside. The restaurant serves
up delectable dishes such as
king prawns with fennel and
confit of duck. The combination
of a modern restaurant serving
up traditional dishes in such as
magnificent setting has grown a
dedicated following.

Can't ski, won't ski? Too much snow or not enough? Find out about **other things to do** in Tignes.

What you'll find in this chapter

Non-skiing activities

Whether bad weather has driven you off the slopes, you don't ski or you simply want a change, there are plenty of activities in Tignes to keep you busy. With everything from adrenaline-fuelled adventures to relaxing in a spa to browsing the shopping on offer, there should never be a boring moment.

Art & Exhibitions
Heritage Centre
T +33 (0)4 79 40 04 40
Le Lac, Maison de Tignes, 4–7pm or (in bad weather: 2–7pm), closed Saturdays, free entry.
The original village of Tignes lies under the Lac du Chevril. See and hear the emotional story of how the villagers were forced to abandon their homes and how a great ski resort was born from it. Temporary exhibitions are also held here (➤ 9).

Bowling
Jacks Club Bowling
T +33 (0)4 79 06 39 95
Le Lac, entrance on road towards Val Claret, 12pm – 2am.
Bowling, games arcade, pool table, Sky TV and bar.

Cinema
Cine Claret
T +33 (0)4 79 06 66 62
W snowtrap.com
Val Claret centre, on the left as you arrive in the upper level on the road, screenings at 6pm and 9pm (at 2.30pm in bad weather).
English films are advertised VOST (original version with French sub-titles). Cinema listings are shown on posters throughout the resort and on leaflets in all the tourist offices.

Climbing
Evolution 2
T +33 (0)4 79 06 43 78
W evolution2.com
Le Lac, Palafour, from €89.
Practise climbing frozen ice walls in Tignes and progress onto the huge frozen waterfall on the road to Val d'Isère.

Tignespace
T +33 (0)4 79 40 04 40
Le Lac, entrance on road towards Val Claret, 4.30–8.30pm except Saturday, €7.20.
Indoor climbing (insurance compulsory including carre neige ➤ 22).

You can also have lessons from the Bureau des Guides (> 31).

Dog sledding
Evolution 2
T +33 (0)4 79 06 43 78
W evolution2.com
Le Lac, Palafour, from €45.
Brilliant for zooming around the frozen lake hanging onto your hat as the excited dogs take off after the nearest marmotte.

Flights
Aeroclub de Palet
T +33 (0)4 79 06 57 60
Pleasure flights and mountain aviation courses. Trips from €100.

Gym & health and beauty
Altitude Spa
T +33 (0)4 79 06 34 36
W campanules.com
Le Lac Rosset, Les Campanules Hotel, entry from €30.
Hotel spa with hydro-jet baths, sauna and spa treatments.

Les Bains du Montana
T +33 (0)4 79 40 01 44
W vmontana.com
Le Lac les Almes, Village Montana, entry from €20.
Hotel spa with swimming pool, wellness area, spa treatments and a gym.

Centre Spa and Mountain Beauty
T +33 (0)4 79 40 22 50
Val Claret, Grande Motte, from €25.
Swimming pool, aquagym, gym, sauna and beauty treatments.

Le Lagon leisure centre
T +33 (0)4 79 40 04 40
W tignes.net
Le Lac, by the lake, 11am-9pm, Saturday: 3-7pm, swimming and spa: €13 per day.
The new leisure centre is the pride of the resort with a twenty-five metre swimming pool, a play pool with a water slide, a children's pool, a large spa area and a gym.

Tignespace
T +33 (0)4 79 40 04 40
W tignes.net
Le Lac, entrance on road to Val Claret, 4.30-8.30pm except Saturday.
Basketball, football, volleyball, tennis, squash, climbing.

Helicopter flights
Evolution 2
T +33 (0)4 79 06 43 78
W evolution2.com
Le Lac, Palafour, from €30.
Pleasure flights and heli-skiing
(> 30).

Horse riding
Evolution 2
T +33 (0)4 79 06 43 78
W evolution2.com
Le Lac, Palafour, from €28 for
adults, from €8 for children.
Ride one of the sturdy mountain
ponies around the lake at sunset
with a vin chaud break to give
you enough energy to race the
others back.

Ice diving
Evolution 2
T +33 (0)4 79 06 43 78
W evolution2.com
Le Lac, Palafour, from €70.
For a truly surreal experience,
go scuba diving underneath the
frozen lake. Wearing two jumpers
under the dry suit keeps you
warm but the still quiet water
underneath the ice can make for
an eerie dive.

Ice driving
Evolution 2
T +33 (0)4 79 06 43 78
W evolution2.com
Le Lac, Palafour, from €25.

Snow Driver Tignes
T +33 (0)6 08 06 67 22
Circuit glace, Les Brévières.

Ice Grotto
Grotte de Glace
Val Claret, Grande Motte glacier,
access via the Funicular, adults
€4, children €3.
Take a tour in this stunning ice
cave – 200m of tunnel dug deep
into the glacier filled with ice
sculptures.

Ice skating
Le Lac, Tignes lake, 2-7.30pm
(Saturday: 2-6pm), ice skate
rental: €3 for adults, €2 for
children.
Skate on the frozen lake in Tignes
– one path for cross-country and a
rink for skating.

Library
T +33 (0)4 79 40 09 89
Le Lac, Monday to Friday:
6-8pm.

Multimedia
Orange Tignes Multimedia
T +33 (0)4 79 40 04 40
W tignes.net
Le Lac, Maison de Tignes,
(top floor), Sunday to Friday:
4.30-8.30pm (opens at 2pm in
bad weather).
Computer games, video editing,
photo downloading, computers with
internet, printers, fax machine and
Wi-Fi – everything you need. Games
evening on Thursday from 8.30-
10.30pm (book though the centre).
You can also access the Wi-Fi
anywhere in the Maison de Tignes.

Paragliding
This is a must-try activity. Ski off
the side of a cliff up on the Tovière
mountain and swoop around the
skies over the resort until you float
back down to the lake.

Evolution 2
T +33 (0)4 79 06 43 78
W evolution2.com
Le Lac, Palafour, €70.

Snocool
T +33 (0)4 79 40 08 58
Le Lac, Rue de la Poste.

Tignes Paragliding School
T +33 (0)6 09 40 05 74

Skidooing
Definitely worth a try, skidooing
involves driving a snowmobile round
the mountains looking rather cool.
Night-time adventures available.

Ecole de Motoneige de Tignes
T +33 (0)6 07 10 19 62

Evolution 2
T +33 (0)4 79 06 43 78
W evolution2.com
Le Lac, Palafour, from €44 for the
driver, €18 for passenger.

Sledging
T +33 (0)4 79 40 04 40, *€3.70.*
Take the kids or have a go yourself
on the purpose-built run next
to the Grande Motte or on the
nursery slopes around resort.

Snow shoeing
Guided walks start from about €50
but details of walking routes are
available from the tourist office.
Alternatively, the local Tabacs (**>** 101)
generally have a good selection of
walking guides (although they may
not be in English).

Bureau des Guides
T +33 (0)4 79 06 42 76
W guidesdetignes.com
Val Claret centre.

Evolution 2
T +33 (0)4 79 06 43 78
W evolution2.com
Le Lac, Palafour.

Swimming
See Gym & health and beauty
(> 94).

Trampolines
These bungee trampolines are
suitable for children over three
years of age. They open around
4pm (earlier later on in the season)
and cost €5 per go.

F.Dufour
T +33 (0)6 09 47 63 95
Le Lac, by Maison de Tignes.

S.Ribaudeau
T +33 (0)6 71 46 05 34
Le Lavachet, behind bus stop.

Video hire
Snow Video
T +33 (0)4 79 06 27 87
Le Lavachet, Hameau de Tovière.
Rent DVDs, TVs and DVD players
from this shop. You can also buy
games, videos and accessories.

Walks
See snow shoeing (> 96).

Yoga classes
Charlotte Saint Jean
T +33 (0)6 03 10 63 95
Le Haut des Brévières.

Other events
See the weekly Tignes *Animations*
guide for what's on during your stay.

It also has details of activities on offer during bad weather. Pick up a copy from any of the tourist offices (> 123).

Shopping

Tignes' main shopping hotspots are in Val Claret centre and Le Lac. Lower down, Les Boisses only has a few shops but it is in chairlift/skiing distance of Les Brévières which has more local amenities.

Opening hours

Shops tend to open quite early in the morning (about 8am) and close for lunch (until 2/4pm). They then reopen until around 7pm. Unless specified otherwise, the shops listed in this chapter follow that pattern. The exception to the rule are ski hire shops, which tend to stay open all day at weekends.

Bakery *(Boulangerie)*

One of the best things about France is the fabulous range of bread and pastries available. Browse in these bread shops and try a 'boule de campagne' (round country loaf) or 'pain complet' (wholemeal bread) instead of a standard baguette and pick up a dessert from the many intricately made sweets on offer.

Chalet du Pain

Val Claret centre, 7.15am – 12.45pm, 4.30 – 7.30pm.
Le Lac Rosset, 7am – 8pm.

Chardon Bleu Patisserie

Le Lac, Palafour, 7am – 1pm, 3 – 8pm.

Le Choucas

Lavachet, to right of Sherpa, 7am – 1pm, 4 – 7.30pm.

Sherpa

Les Brévières, main street, 7am-1pm, 4-7.30pm.

Ski clothing and equipment

Most ski hire shops also sell clothing and equipment (> 40).

Supermarkets, butchers and delicatessens

The majority of the supermarkets in Tignes open from 8.30am until around 1pm and then from 4pm to 7.30/8pm. Each year, there will be one that will stay open all day

– check with the tourist office. To supplement your purchases, there are delicatessens all over Tignes selling traditional Savoie fare including sauccisse (dried flavoured sausage), local cheese and vin de Savoie (the local wine). Wander in and ask for a taste of something *(un degustation)* and see what you think.

Val Claret
La Grange

T +33 (0)4 79 06 37 96
Val Claret centre.
Selling local produce such as cheese, cured meats, tinned goods and bread. Also selling regional decoration, beauty products and souvenirs.

Sherpa
T +33 (0)4 79 06 30 74
Val Claret centre.
This branch has a separate shop
for the butchers and deli and then
the bakery is in the main shop.
There is another smaller branch
by the Grande Motte.

Le Lac
Palette de Boulélé
T +33 (0)4 79 08 52 12
Le Rosset.
Regional products such as
cheeses and meats as well as a
cosy little wine bar at the back
where you can sample some of
their wine and cheese – much
recommended!

SPAR
T +33 (0)4 79 06 52 09
Palafour.
This is the biggest (and priciest)
supermarket in resort although its
fresh produce is a lot better than
the others. As well as the main
supermarket there is a butchers,
deli and bakery. They also have a
local produce section that is ideal
for presents. Free delivery of your
shopping if you spend over €50.

Le Lavachet
Sherpa
T +33 (0)4 79 06 31 41
Centre.
As well as the supermarket, there
is now a butchers and deli in this
branch.

Les Brévières
Sherpa
T +33 (0)4 79 06 38 64
Main road.

Newsagents and tobacconists *(Tabacs)*
You can buy a selection of UK newspapers in most Tabacs.

La Musardiere
Val Claret centre.

Presse/tabac
Val Claret Grande Motte.

Librarie presse *Le Lac Palafour (not closed for lunch).*

Maison de la Presse
Le Lac Le Rosset.

Tabac Presse *Le Lavachet.*

Echo des Brévières
Les Brévières.

Markets
There is a market along Le Lac Rosset on Sundays and Thursdays selling clothing, local produce and sweets – some stalls can be expensive.

Pharmacy
Pharmacie de Lac
T +33 (0)4 79 06 31 21
Le Lac, Rue de La Poste, 9am – 7.30pm.

Pharmacie du Val Claret
T +33 (0)4 79 06 36 22
Val Claret centre, inside the shopping arcade opposite the Sherpa, 9am – 7.30pm.

Photography
You will find photographers at the top of many lifts, on the terraces of restaurants and in restaurants during the evening. They will take your photo with no obligation to buy. Simply go to the location on the card they hand you and you can buy your photo if you like it. Prices are around €25 for an A4 size photo.

Other things to do

Scott Dunn

Exceptional family ski holidays

The most important part of the family ski holiday formula is
making sure the younger members of your group are happy.
If they're happy you'll be happy.

We offer excellent childcare in all our alpine resorts - Courchevel
1850, Méribel, St Anton, Val d'Isère and Zermatt. And this year sees
the launch of OurSpace, a dedicated winter children's club in
Val d'Isère for our younger guests aged between 4 months
and 13 years.

Having children does not mean the end of the adventure,
if anything, as I'm sure you've realised, it is just the beginning.

Call our ski team now on **020 8682 5050**
or visit **www.scottdunn.com/ski**

Skiing with **children**... dream or nightmare? With a little planning, it can be your best ski holiday ever.

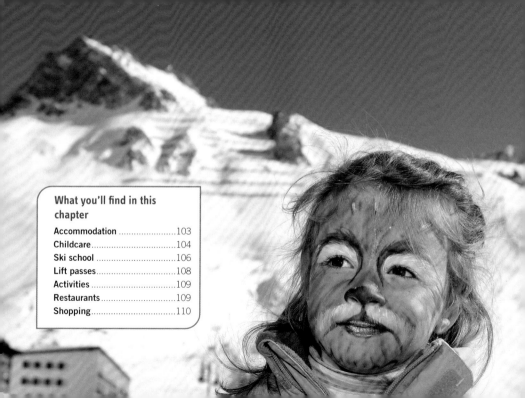

What you'll find in this chapter

Whether you want ski lessons with lunch included or all day care for a baby then this chapter has the answers for you.

Most parents will require some form of childcare during a skiing holiday in order to give them the freedom to explore the pistes at your own pace. Don't forget though that good childcare is hard to find and if you are visiting resort during English school holidays then we'd advise booking early to avoid disappointment.

Accommodation

There certainly isn't a shortage of child-friendly options available in Tignes but it is worth considering the following when booking:

Location is probably the most important consideration especially when you have to get young children to ski school by 9am each morning. A long walk up a steep hill at the end of the day is no fun with tired children. The resort bus stops right on the piste in Le Lac which is perfect for the ski school meeting point so if you are staying in Lavachet or Le Lac this is where you should arrange for lessons to take place. If you are staying in Val Claret or Les Chartreux area then Val Claret is the most central place for lessons.

Considering the accessibility to your accommodation is vital when taking small children on holiday. If you will be using a buggy to transport small children around you may want to know how many steps there are into the building and which floor you will be staying on. Apartment blocks with over four storeys often provide a lift but it may not always be working.

Mealtimes can sometimes be a worry for parents and if this is the case self-catering is always the best bet as it offers you the opportunity to provide your choice of meals when you like. Both hotels and catered chalets will provide an evening meal for children but you will have to eat out during the day.

Children's checklist
- Are items such as cots (and bedding), high chairs, children's cutlery and baby monitors provided? If not who can provide them?
- Is there room for an extra bed or cot to be added to the parent's room?
- Can high tea be arranged for the children?
- Are the children's rooms located away from the often noisy communal area?
- Can different dietary requirements be met?
- Does the company provide its own childcare service?
- Can the company pre-book ski school?

- If the accommodation is a long walk to the lifts, does the company provide transport?

Child-friendly tour operators
These companies are well-known for their focus on families and offer their own programmes. Other operators may give you free child places or discounted/free ski hire.

Crystal
T +44 (0)870 160 6040
W crystalski.co.uk

Mark Warner
T +44 (0)870 770 4228
W markwarner.co.uk

Ski Esprit
T +44 (0)1253 618 300
W esprit-holidays.co.uk

Childcare

Tignesie Tots
T +44 (0)20 8675 1548
W tignesie-tots.com

A private British-run nanny service offering qualified and experienced nannies. Their flexible approach means you can book one of their nannies full or part time and/or evenings. All staff are fully vetted and details about the nannies can be found on their website. Prices vary per hour depending on the number of children you have but you receive a 25% discount when you book a full time nanny.

uality Childcare in Tignes

*Enjoy the fun and beauty of the Alps
safe in the knowledge that your
children are having just as much fun...
if not more!*

gnesie Tots provides a **personal**
nd **flexible** approach combined
with a **wealth of experience**,
owledge and a **love of children**
to give your kids a safe,
fun-packed week full of
adventures.

For information on activities,
ski schools, accommodation and
much more please see our website.

Tignesie
Tots

ww.tignesie-tots.com   Email: info@tignesie-tots.com   Tel: +44(0)7949 040544

Les Farfadets
T +33 (0)6 89 28 81 50
W lesfarfadets.co.uk.
Another private nanny service with English-speaking nannies, however they do not base any of their nannies in Tignes so you will need to provide them with accommodation.

Ski school
We would recommend that your child is a minimum of four years old before they start to learn to ski in a group lesson. They should be able to communicate their needs with confidence, be reasonably independent and have the strength in their legs to learn to snowplough. Group lessons will often consist of French and English children with a mix of both languages spoken but remember that communicating in French will always be the language of choice unless you book with a British school.

ESF
> 38
The main ski school in Tignes has a variety of children's lessons and they also use the Marmottons ski villages in Val Claret and Le Lac. Groups are divided by age and ability and they offer private as well as group lessons. Make sure you request an English-speaking instructor.

Evolution 2
> 39
Popular with the British market, EV2 employs a good number of English-speaking instructors (although you will need to request one) and runs a variety of different lessons for all ages and abilities.

Les Marmottons
T +33 (0)4 79 06 37 12
 (Val Claret)
T +33 (0)4 79 06 51 67 *(Le Lac)*
W marmottons-tignes.com
Based in Le Lac and Val Claret, they take children from as young as three years old in groups of 8-10. They have a sectioned-off ski area on the piste with small drags that is kitted out like a nursery. Bouncy castles and outdoor play equipment is also available to the children. A snack break is taken halfway through

the session; water is provided but ensure your child has a snack in their pocket to enjoy. They also offer ski and boot hire.

First day at ski school

- Leave your contact details with the ski school in case they need to contact you
- Be realistic about what your child can achieve on their first day, they may be tired after travelling to resort but some fresh air and exercise can be just the answer
- Not all children enjoy ski school so be prepared to have a back up plan – for child-friendly activities, > 109
- Offer your child a rest in the afternoon at the beginning of the week – learning to ski is hard work
- Supply your child with a 30+SPF sun cream and lip salve, tissues and a snack
- Remember undoing zips with mittens on can be difficult!
- Beginners do not need ski poles (one less thing to carry) but it is recommended that children wear a helmet whilst skiing. This is particularly essential if they progress to using lifts
- Good quality sunglasses or goggles are essential to protect children's sensitive eyes from the sun. They can be bought in resort for around €25
- Take a small rucksack with a spare change of clothes just in case of an accident. A favourite comforter is useful to cheer little ones up
- Ski school can involve a lot of standing around so children can get cold quickly, particularly before the sun has had a chance to warm up the nursery slopes. Good quality clothing is essential to keep children smiling
- Ski passes are free to children under five years of age and the nursery slopes are also free in Tignes – check with your ski school to see if you will need one later in the week
- Try to get your children to drink as much as possible whilst in resort to prevent them becoming dehydrated. Sports bottles usually encourage children to drink more fluids

- Dungaree style salopettes are nice and warm for small children but almost impossible for them to manage when going to the loo. This style of ski wear is not advisable if children are going to ski school.

Child lift pass prices

5-12 years

1/2 day..... €24.50
1 day........ €33
6 days €160
7 days €183.50

Prices are inclusive of carre neige insurance (> 22) and based on the 2006/7 season.

Activities

These suggestions are particularly good for kids but you can find more in the **Other things to do** chapter (> 93).

Bowling
> 93

Horse riding
Evolution 2 has Shetland ponies for smaller children and ponies for older ones (> 95).

Ice skating
Great value skate hire means you can spend the afternoon skating on the frozen lake (> 95).

Playground
Newly built, this children's playground is in the centre of Le Lac and has swings, slide, pirate ship, a rope bridge and more.

However, the snow level does affect what is useable.

Riding the Aeroski and Funicular
Pedestrians and children are allowed to ride the Aeroski gondola and the Funicular train on good weather days. Children under five can travel free and adults can travel on their ski pass. Children will love the chance to go up in the mountains and once at the top why not stop for a drink and a waffle!

Swimming
The new leisure centre is a big hit with the kids. As well as a children's pool, there is a play pool with a slide for older children (> 94). The water temperature is cooler than expected though so be prepared to keep moving!

Sledging
There are designated safe sledging areas in Le Lac and Lavachet which we recommend that you use with children (> 96).

Trampolines
> 97.

Restaurants

Most restaurants in Tignes provide a children's menu which usually comes with chips. One way to get healthier food is to share an adult portion between the children.

Highchairs are hard to find so it is worth taking a strap on booster seat or sitting outside in the buggy works just as well. It is advisable to

Children

go prepared with cutlery, beaker, bib and wipes as a large knife and fork complete with a glass tumbler can make lunch times rather stressful!

Chalet du Pain
> 99

Le Coffee – Evolution 2
> 67

Escale Blanche
> 69

La Pignatta
> 67

Saint Jacques
> 68

Mountain restaurants

Most restaurants in Tignes ski area have a self-service section offering up food such as pasta, pizzas and burgers. We'd recommend the places below as particularly child-friendly as you can get down to resort easily from them, either by ski lift or by just a short slope.

Alpage
> 85

Chalet du Bollin
> 85

Panoramic
> 85

Tovière
> 86

Shopping

Food and baby items

You can purchase Pampers and Grand Jury nappies in all of the supermarkets (> 99) in Tignes as well as baby wipes and swim nappies although you won't find brands of formula milk that you recognise such as SMA or Aptimil so always bring your own. Jars of baby food can also be bought in the supermarket but there isn't much choice so you may want to bring some from the UK or ask your chalet staff or hotel kitchen staff to whizz something up for you. For any dietary requirements, the supermarkets are now stocking a number of 'free from' foods but it is always advisable to bring as much with you as possible to stick with what you know.

If you are driving to resort you can always stop in Bourg Saint Maurice where there is a large Super U that offers a much bigger range of children's items as well as 'free from' foods.

Pharmacies

These are great for supplying medicines such as Calpol, conjunctivitis drops and nappy creams. Most items are available over the counter without the need of a prescription (> 102).

Toy shops

There are a number of Tabacs (> 101) selling toys, colouring books or for something a little nicer visit Bricolac situated on Le Rosset opposite the nursery slope in Le Lac.

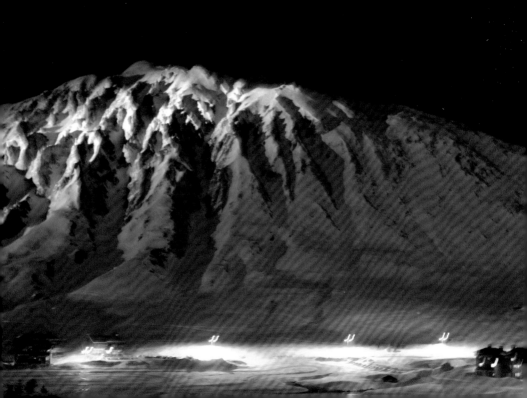

The list – sounds boring but it has all the important information that you don't need until you need it...

Notes

- Telephone numbers include the international dialling code. From Tignes, drop the 00 33 and dial the number using the (0)

- We use local landmarks and main streets as points of reference. Locations of these are shown on ➤ 8, 124 and 125.

- You can pick up a resort map from any of the Maison de Tignes.

Banks and cashpoints

The banks can be found in the main shopping areas of Val Claret and Le Lac. All banks are closed at the weekend. You will also find cashpoints in the main shopping areas.

Credit Agricole

Val Claret centre and upper level of Maison de Tignes in Le Lac.
Both branches have a cashpoint although the Le Lac one is on the outside of the Maison de Tignes building.

Banque Populaire des Alpes

Next to Intersport in Le Lac and Les Brévières.
Both branches have a cashpoint.

La Poste

Val Claret centre and Le Lac, Rue de la Poste.
Both branches of the Post Office have cashpoints.

Buses

Free ski buses run between Le Lavachet, Le Lac and Val Claret throughout the day from 8am-8pm. After 8pm, they run every half an hour until midnight after which they run every hour.

From 9pm, the buses detour up to the centre of Val Claret (except Saturdays) stopping opposite the games arcade and outside Club Med. You can find bus timetables at every bus stop.

Free buses run between Les Boisses and Maison de Tignes in Le Lac every half hour with the first bus starting at 8am from Les Boisses. The last bus leaves Le Lac at 6.45pm. In the evening, three further buses leave Le Lac at 8.30pm, 10pm and midnight.

During the day you can also use the free chairlift between Les Boisses and Les Brévières.

There are buses during the day that go to Val d'Isère and Bourg Saint Maurice – look in the tourist offices for times and fares.

Car hire

The nearest places to hire a car is Europcar in Bourg Saint Maurice and Val; they can also arrange to deliver your car to Tignes. For all other car hire companies > 20.

Car parks

The resort tries hard to make it a car-free place and has plenty of parking available in each village. The flipside of this is that the resort police are tough on illegal parking so your best bet is to park your car at the start of the week and then leave it there until you leave.

Val Claret
Parking du Val Claret
946 indoor spaces

Parking de la Grande Motte
750 outdoor spaces

Le Lac
Parking du Lac
1255 indoor spaces

Le Lavachet
Parking du Lavachet
325 indoor spaces

Les Boisses and Les Brévières
Free car parks in both villages

Chemist

> 101

Churches

There are churches in Le Lac and Les Boisses; details of services can be found in the tourist offices. The church in Les Boisses is a replica of the original church from the old village of Tignes, now hidden under the Lac du Chevril.

Credit Cards

Although payment by credit card is commonplace, many French establishments (especially restaurants) do not accept American Express. You will need to have a PIN number to use both credit and debit cards in France.

Dentist

Cabinet Dentaire
T: +33 (0)4 79 04 19 58
Palafour (lakeside), Le Lac.

Dry Cleaning

Au Lavoir du Lac
T: +33 (0)4 79 06 32 01
Le Lac, Palafour (lakeside).
There are self-service laundrettes in Val Claret, Le Lac and Le Lavachet > 119.

Electricity

Voltage in France is 220 volts, so you may find that some appliances don't work. You will need a two pin plug or an adaptor. If you forget your adaptor, they are available in all the supermarkets for about €5.

Emergency numbers

Medical emergency: 15 or 112
(from mobile)
Fire Brigade: 18
Police:
+33 (0)4 79 40 04 93
Gendarmerie:
+33 (0)4 79 06 32 06
Ambulance:
+33 (0)4 79 06 59 18
Piste security:
+33 (0)4 79 06 32 00
Car breakdown:
+33 (0)4 79 06 35 56

For medical centre and hospital
> 119.

Environment

Around the resort you will notice
poubelle signs. These are the
rubbish bins. Generally you will find
three bins next to each other for
recycling purposes, one for general
rubbish, one for glass and one for
plastics. Look out for small wooden
huts around resort – these are for
recycling cardboard and boxes.

There are also ashtrays at the
top of the ski lifts to deposit your
cigarette butts.

Events

There is a free weekly leaflet called
'Animations' which can be found in
most bars, hotels and restaurants.
It schedules forthcoming events
around the resort. There is also
a channel on television which
advertises the week's events.
English mag, The Mountain
Echo is well worth picking up for
entertainment listings, reviews and
articles. Pick it up from bars or the
tourist offices.

Rubbish

There is always a tremendous amount of rubbish on the slopes when the snow melts – don't add to it! A single cigarette butt contains 4,000 toxic substances and can pollute up to 1.3m³ of snow – under any one chairlift there could be up to 30,000 butts.

How long does rubbish last?

Plastic bottle: 100-1000 years
Aluminium cans: 100-500 years
Cigarette stubs: 2-7 years
Fruit peel: 3 days – 6 months
Paper: 100-500 years
Sweet wrappers: 100-450 years

Source: mountain-riders.org

The Ski Club of Great Britain runs a **Respect the Mountain** (respectthemountain.com) campaign to safeguard the environment and the long-term future of skiing.

Garages

Amandine Auto

T +33 (0)4 79 06 35 56
Le Lac, opposite the Maison de Tignes.

This garage is the only one in resort which makes it quite pricey. However, it is useful for emergencies and also sells fuel and snow chains, although it is always cheaper to get these in Bourg Saint Maurice.

Hardware

The supermarkets around the resort all sell basic maintenance equipment. For more specialised equipment there is a hardware store in the Le Rosset side of Le Lac called Bric-o-Lac.

Health

A few tips to keep you healthy on holiday:

- The sun is much stronger at altitude – make sure you wear sun cream, even on overcast days.
- You need to drink at least three times as much water to keep hydrated at altitude – more if you're topping up with wine and beer! Your muscles are the first part of your body to dehydrate so you'll suffer less aches and pains if you keep hydrated.
- Good sunglasses are a must to prevent watering eyes and snow blindness.
- Lip salves with a high sun protection factor will prevent unattractive chapped lips!

Internet

Many places in Tignes now offer free internet for customers or paid-for Wi-Fi and computers linked up to the internet. This is a selection:

Val Claret
Couloir > 76
Drop Zone > 77

Le Lac
Alpaka > 78
Jam Bar > 79
Orange Multimedia centre > 96

Le Lavachet
Brasero > 79
Lavachet Lounge > 79

Les Brévières
Underground Bar > 80

Key cutting

Au Lavoir du Lac

T 04 79 06 32 01

Le Lac, Palafour building.

Language

Although many of the people working in shops and restaurants speak English, a little French goes a long way. Don't be discouraged if they answer you back in English! See our table opposite which sets out useful phrases.

Useful phrases:	
Hello	Bonjour
Goodbye	Au revoir
How are you?	Comment ça va?
Please	S'il vous plait
Thank-you	Merci
Excuse me/sorry	Excusez-moi
How much…?	C'est combien?
The bill please	L'addition, s'il vous plait
Jug of tap water	Un carafe d'eau
Snowboard	Snowboard
Skis	Les skis
Ski/boarding boots	Chaussures des ski/surf ski/ boarding boots
Ski poles	Batons
Lift pass	Forfait
I am lost	Je suis perdu
Where is the nearest lift/ restaurant?	Ou est le télésiège/restaurant le plus près?
Help!	Au secours!
Watch out!	Attention!

Launderettes

All machines accept euro coins: save your coins as it is sometimes hard to get change from the nearby shops. In general allow for €4 per wash (or €7 for a large machine) and €1 for six minutes of dryer-time.

Val Claret
Inside the Sefcotel building.

Le Lac
In the Palafour building, lakeside. They also do service washes.

Le Lavachet
Inside Hameau de Toviere.

Lost property

Lost property that has been handed in can be reclaimed from the STGM lift pass office, the tourist office or the Police Municipal in Le Lac. Before going to any of these places, check with the nearest lift attendant as this is often where people hand things in.

Medical

For any medical treatment, take your insurance documents and your EHIC (old E111) with you. Many doctors and the medical centres in Tignes are private so they will often ask you to pay for all medical care upfront. If you are unable to do this, contact your medical assistance company, which should be marked on your insurance policy, they may be able to send a payment guarantee.

If you have to have to be admitted into hospital, contact your insurance company immediately so they can fax payment confirmation direct to the hospital. If you are not insured you will have to pay for everything which can be very expensive. If you visit the hospital it is unlikely you will be charged but it is advised that you take your passport with you, as they may need a copy.

Cabinet Medical Val Claret
T +33 (0)4 79 06 59 64
Val Claret, upper level opposite Hotel Curling, Monday to Saturday: 9am-12pm, 3-7pm, Sunday: 10am-12pm, 4-7pm.

Cabinet Medical Le Lac
T +33 (0)4 79 06 50 07
Far end of Palafour building lakeside, Le Lac, Monday to

Saturday: 9am–12pm, 3–7pm,
Sunday: 10am–12pm, 4–7pm.

Hôpital de Bourg
T +33 (0)4 79 41 79 79
Bourg Saint Maurice.

Money
All prices in this guide are in euro unless indicated otherwise. See also banks and cashpoints ➤ 113.

Optician
SOS Optique
Val Claret centre, opposite the Sherpa and Le Lac, Rue de la Poste.

Parking
➤ 113

Pharmacy
➤ 101

Physiotherapists
Cabinet de Kinésithérapie-Ostéopathie
T +33 (0)4 79 06 48 95
Le Lac, far end of Palafour building lakeside.

Police
The Police (Gendarmerie) station is located about 100m from the petrol station in Le Lac along the road out of Tignes. If you get your car towed, go to the Police Municipale on the right of the petrol station to get it back. For information on reporting lost property to the Police ➤ 119.

Post Offices
You don't need to go to the Post Office to buy stamps; most places selling postcards will also sell stamps to the UK. These normally cost about €0.60. Letters take around four working days to arrive. Post boxes are pale yellow and usually fixed to the wall rather than free-standing.

There are three La Postes in Tignes and, in general, they are open 9am–12pm and 1–5.30pm. On Saturdays they are open from 8.30-11am.
Val Claret in the Sefcotel building
Le Lac Rue de la Poste
Les Brevieres in the tourist office

Radio

92.2 and 88.2fm is R'Tignes, the local radio station. Roughly four times a day there are weather reports, resort information and news in English.

Rubbish

> 116

Safety

Ski resorts are traditionally a relatively safe place to holiday. Most crime involves theft so ensure you keep your belongings with you in the bar (especially your ski jacket and/or lift pass) and also keep your accommodation locked at all times.

You should also get into the habit of swapping skis with your companions so you leave mismatched pairs outside restaurants and bars. Theft is more of a problem in resort or where there is pedestrian access back into resort (by gondolas for example). You can also buy a ski lock for around €10-15.

Ski lockers

There are ski lockers in almost all residential building in Tignes. Most building also have a rule that you are not allowed to wear your ski boots within the building.

Sun

Always remember to wear a high factor sun cream or protective clothing when you go out in the sun, even if the sun doesn't seem very hot. The rays are very powerful at high-altitude and the weather can often by deceiving; usually you won't realise you are burnt until the evening.

Taxis

It is difficult to get a taxi to take you around resort unless you want to travel between Les Boisses or Les Brévières. Most companies do airport transfers journeys to the airport and train station and some will also go to Val d'Isère. It costs about €20 one way to Les Boisses and €40 one way to Val d'Isère from the upper villages.

See > 22 for taxi companies.

Toilets

Val Claret
Grande Motte – between car park and bus stop area.

Grande Motte
In Funicular station Maison de Tignes.

Le Lac
Maison de Tignes

Le Lavachet
Maison de Tignes

TV Cable

Tignes Cable
T +33 (0)4 79 06 31 27
Val Claret, Maison de Tignes.
Get it for one day, one week, one month or a year (English channels: BBC Prime, BBC World and Eurosport). Look out for Tignes TV with all the resort information for the week on it.

Water

Drink plenty of water because at high-altitude you dehydrate much faster. If you have aching legs, one of the causes of this is that you need more water so take a bottle out on the slopes with you.

The tap water is drinkable in Tignes. If you ask for water with a meal you will be served mineral water, which you must pay for. If you ask for a *'carafe d'eau'*, a carafe of natural water, you will usually be given tap water – which is free.

Weather

Generally you can expect January and February to be colder than March and April. December is less snow-sure (but correspondingly cheaper, except at Christmas).

In recent years, there has been a later heavy snowfall in April and, as this is the cheapest time of year (barring Easter holidays), it can be well worth the gamble.

You can find the daily Meteo France forecast in the lift stations and tourist offices.

On **maddogski.com,** you can find daily snow reports, weather forecasts and webcams for Tignes.

Many businesses, especially ski schools and hotels, display the weather forecast on their notice boards or front desks.

Tourist office - Maison de Tignes

T +33 (0)4 79 40 04 40
W www.tignes.net
The main office is in the large
wooden Maison de Tignes
building in the middle of
Le Lac. Opening hours: Sunday
to Friday: 8.30am-7pm,
Saturdays: 8am-8pm.

- General information
- Car parking reception desk
- Autocars Martin bus/SNCF
  desk
- Tignes reservations
- Orange multimedia centre
- STGM lift pass desk and
  vending machine
- Heritage centre
- Showers and toilets

- Credit Agricole bank and
  cashpoint

The **Val Claret** office is found
in the Nevada building and is
open the same hours as the Le
Lac office.

- General information
- STGM lift pass office
- Autocars Martin bus
- Left luggage
- Showers and toilets
- Bureau Tignes TV cable office

Le Lavachet office is found next
to the underground parking and
is open: Friday 9am to Monday
6am non-stop, all other days
from 10am-6pm.

- General information
- Car park reception desk
- Left luggage
- Showers and toilets
- STGM lift pass desk

Les Brévières office, see website
for opening hours

- General information
- ESF ski school
- Post Office
- STGM lift pass desk

Les Boisses
- General information
  (Saturday only)
- STGM lift pass desk
  (Saturdays, Sundays and
  Mondays)

Tignes – Le Lac

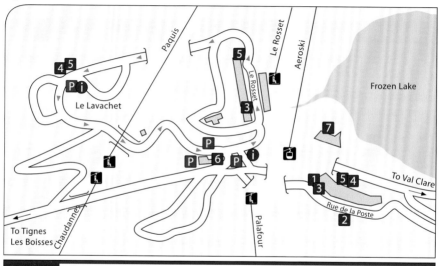

Key:

- **ⓘ** Maison de Tignes
- **P** Parking

1. Palafour shopping arcade
2. Post Office
3. Tabacs

4. Supermarkets
5. Bakeries
6. Garage

7. Le Lagon leisure centre

Tignes – Val Claret

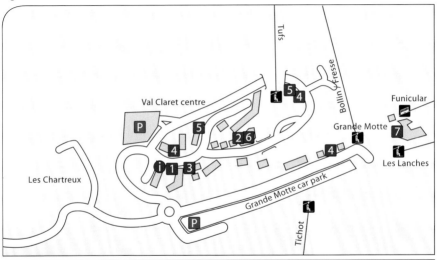

Key:

- **ℹ** Maison de Tignes
- **P** Parking

1. Le Nevada
2. Post Office
3. Tabac
4. Supermarkets
5. Bakeries
6. Sefcotel building
7. STGM main office

Index

A

maddogski.com

And finally…

We would like to thank the following people for their help and support: Susie Aust, Bird, Phillip Blackwell, Matt Cooke, Clare Dawson, Kim Davidson, Carrie Hainge at the Ski Club of Great Britain, Sarah Hookes, Penny Harding, Paddi Hutchins-Clarke, Juliet Johnston, Simon Milton, Louise Moore, Rachel Thomas, Richard Williamson.

Do you know something we don't? Jot down your tips and recommendations and let us know about them at info@maddogski.com

_____

_____

_____

_____

_____

_____

_____